Passover
Encounter

EXPERIENCING YOUR PERSONAL EXODUS

Passover
Encounter

EXPERIENCING YOUR PERSONAL EXODUS

By Boaz Michael

FIRST FRUITS OF
ZION

Proclaiming the Torah and its way
of life, fully centered on Messiah,
to today's People of God

Publisher freely grants permission to reproduce short quotations in reviews, magazines, newspapers, Web sites or other publications. To reproduce, transmit or photocopy more than 400 words, please secure permission in writing from the publisher, which will be granted upon written request.

First Edition 2005
Printed in the United States of America

ISBN: 1-892124-20-3

Unless otherwise noted, Scripture quotations are taken from the New American Standard Bible®, Copyright © 1960, 1962, 1963, 1968, 1971, 1972, 1973, 1975, 1977, 1995 by The Lockman Foundation. Used by permission (*www.Lockman.org*). The author substituted "Messiah" for "Christ" and "Yeshua" for "Jesus" with permission from the Lockman Foundation.

Haggadah developed by: Boaz Michael
Design by: Avner Wolff

ATTENTION CHURCHES, SYNAGOGUES, STUDY GROUPS, TEACHERS AND OTHER ORGANIZATIONS: Quantity discounts are available on bulk purchases of this book for educational, fundraising, or event purposes. Special books or book excerpts can also be created to fit specific needs. For more information, please contact First Fruits of Zion, PO Box 620099, Littleton, CO, 80162–0099. Phone (303) 933–2119 or (800) 775–4807.

First Fruits of Zion

PO Box 620099
Littleton, Colorado 80162–0099 USA
Phone (303) 933–2119 or (800) 775–4807
Fax (303) 933–0997
www.ffoz.org

Comments and questions: *feedback@ffoz.org*

And you shall observe this event as an
ordinance for you and your children forever.

When you enter the land which
the LORD will give you, as He has promised,
you shall observe this rite.

And when your children say to you,
"What does this rite mean to you?"
you shall say, "It is a Passover sacrifice to
the LORD who passed over the houses of the
sons of Israel in Egypt when He smote the
Egyptians, but spared our homes."

And the people bowed low and worshiped.

Exodus 12:24–27

Acknowledgments

My confidence to put forth this Haggadah has been greatly enhanced by knowing that this process truly works. Each year, I have seen my wife and four children examine their lives, cry out to God and realize true and lasting deliverance from areas of flesh. Thank you for being such a wonderful and supportive family. I love each of you dearly.

A special thank you to all the editors, reviewers, and proof readers who helped create this resource. It thrilled my heart to hear all of your comments about how Messiah-centered this Haggadah is…which leads me to its dedication:

I dedicate this work to You, my Master, my Messiah, to You I have given my life in the service of building Your Kingdom.

Come soon!

Contents

Foreword

This instructional Passover booklet (*Haggadah*) is the result of years of heartfelt searching and discovery. While there are many different types and styles of Passover *Haggadot* available in Jewish synagogues, Messianic congregations, and churches, the goal of this book is to cause individuals everywhere, whatever their spiritual understanding or background, to evaluate, experience, and grow in their faith through the observance of God's appointed time of Passover.

The more thoroughly that we understand the Exodus, the greater our understanding will be of how the God of Israel sanctifies, delivers, and equips. Let us then approach this time and season with our hearts and minds prepared to encounter our Maker in a significant and meaningful way.

The cover of this *Haggadah* aptly illustrates the marked growth that we all experience in our spiritual walk with the Lord. In the background, we recognize the golden haze of the past life of sin in Egypt. But as we yield ourselves to His sanctification process, we come into fresh new life, pictured by the green, fruit-bearing branches of the tree.

This *Haggadah* is intended to be a message of hope. If we pray and cry out to be free, God will answer our prayers. May this encounter make this a reality.

In Messiah,
Boaz Michael
PRESIDENT, FIRST FRUITS OF ZION

Overview

The Hebrew term given to God's appointed times is *moadim*. These are spiritual appointments with God. They commemorate history, but they also make history. They make our history. Whenever we honor one of the *moadim*,[1] the same spiritual forces that were present at their inauguration are expressed and reflected in the private world of our souls. They define our individual futures and retrospectively our corporate history as the people of God. His *moadim* mold us and shape us into His sanctified people as they form the very shadow of our Redeemer.[2] God's *moadim* were given to heal, mature, and sanctify us.

As the redeemed people of God—through the work of His servant, our Messiah—the appointed time of Passover provides an opportunity for us to put off the 'old man' by leaving our weaknesses behind in 'Egypt.' When viewed as a composite group, the appointed times can be instruments through which the Creator sanctifies and spiritually matures His children annually. Participation in this cycle allows us to experience new levels of freedom and growth—breaking free from bondage to sinful habits.

This maturation process entails that we spiritually prepare to meet with God at His appointed times, that we prepare to be attentive to the work of His Spirit as we meet with Him, and that we determine to set our minds on things of righteousness. As we do this, we begin a process in which we choose to agree with God and obey Him in all things, thus actively participating in the process of crucifying our flesh. For a time, our flesh may resist the Spirit, and even war with it, but we will grow stronger as we eagerly cooperate with "putting to death the deeds of the body,"[3]

...because the mind set on the flesh is hostile toward God; for it does not subject itself to the law of God, for it is not even able to do so, and those who are in the flesh cannot please God. (Romans 8:7–8)

Furthermore, as we turn our minds away from the flesh, we become trained to follow the things of the Spirit—God's Law (Torah)—His written, expressed will and wisdom. Due to the redeeming grace afforded us by God, our minds, when set on things of the Spirit, will be made subject to the teachings of Torah. In so doing, we please God because our faith results in actions that agree with His Spirit.

While every believer is made righteous (made right) before God through faith in Messiah Yeshua, we are each sanctified (made holy) through His work in our lives. Obedience to God's whole written Word is how we accept the new creation[4] He has brought about in us. It is the process by which we conform ourselves to the image of His Son—the Living Word. Our obedience to God's commandments causes us to be strengthened and to grow toward maturity.

By faithfully and eagerly observing God's *moadim* each year, we encounter a unique process of sanctification through which we can spiritually mature. This cycle affords us the opportunity to forsake the ways of the flesh that wage war on our spiritual selves. Sin begets sin; obedience begets obedience. Our participation in the *moadim* brings forth change and new fruits of righteousness.

God's calendar begins appropriately in the spring—a time when new life breaks forth. Winter is difficult and full of dormancy, hibernation, and death. With the exception of the weekly *Shabbat*, there are no biblical feasts in the winter. It is a time of silence and introspection. Passover is *chag ha'aviv*, the festival of spring; it is a time historically related with the beginning of revival,[5] renewal, and freedom. It is a time to enter into a renaissance of sorts as we encounter our Maker and find new levels of freedom from the bondage of our personal Egypt or *Mitzrayim*.[6]

In a spiritual sense, every one of us has his own spiritual Egypt. *Mitzrayim*, the Hebrew for Egypt, relates to the Hebrew word *meitzarim*, meaning boundaries and limitations. On Pesach we leave behind the forces which confine our spirits and begin a new phase of divine service.[7]

Through the experience of Passover, believers annually relive Messiah's gift of freedom from bondage. This experience translates into deliverance from sin (leaven) in our lives.

> Your boasting is not good. Do you not know that a little leaven [*chametz*] leavens the whole lump of dough? Clean out the old leaven so that you may be a new lump, just as you are in fact unleavened. For Messiah our Passover also has been sacrificed. Therefore let us celebrate the feast, not with old leaven, nor with the leaven of malice and wickedness, but with the unleavened bread of sincerity and truth. (1 Corinthians 5:6–8)

Complete and final deliverance from sin does not only happen at the moment of our initial salvation through Messiah; rather, it is a continual process in which we can participate each year. God's appointed times keep us focused on this reality and are ever before us, graciously helping us in this process of purging.

> …and put on the new self, which in the likeness of God has been created in righteousness and holiness of the truth. (Ephesians 4:24)

> Do not lie to one another, since you laid aside the old self with its evil practices, and have put on the new self who is being renewed to a true knowledge according to the image of the One who created him… (Colossians 3:9–10)

His appointments, like all of His commandments, are gifts and demonstrations of His love and grace. They are the means by which we see our true reflection—our true and ideal nature—in Messiah.

> But prove yourselves doers of the word, and not merely hearers who delude themselves. For if anyone is a hearer of the word and not a doer, he is like a man who looks at his natural face in a mirror; for once he has looked at himself and gone away, he has immediately forgotten what kind

of person he was. But one who looks intently at the perfect law, the law of liberty, and abides by it, not having become a forgetful hearer but an effectual doer, this man will be blessed in what he does. (James 1:22–25)

Background

I began to honor God's calendar during my young adult years. I have many fond memories of those times. But it took several years for me to more fully understand and yield to the spiritual lessons that the appointed times are meant to teach. In turn, it has taken many years for these truths to become an integral part of my daily, weekly, monthly, and annual spiritual growth.

I first observed this complete annual cycle while living in Israel. During that time, I realized how inattentive I had been to God's calendar. The appointed times always seemed to creep up unannounced. Consequently, I was usually unprepared for these appointments.

In the United States, stores begin marketing holiday items months in advance—they create an atmosphere in order to increase sales. In Israel, preparation for the biblical appointed times and holy days created a similar frenzy. It just so happens that the holidays associated with Israel are those found in the Scriptures. My heightened awareness of the coming holy days and my whole-hearted desire to meet with the Master began impacting my life in deeper and more meaningful ways each year.

Honoring God's *moadim* in the Land created an intrinsic 'spiritual' atmosphere of anticipation unlike anything I had experienced before. In the Land, it is difficult, if not impossible, to ignore the rhythm of the biblical calendar.[8] The appointments of God and the commandments to honor them were continually before me. They are the driving force behind the structure of life in Israel. I believe that this structure is exactly what God intended when He established His unconditional, eternal calendar.

I learned and am continuing to learn very powerful lessons through these experiences. God's appointed times, outlined in Leviticus 23, were not intended to be mere historic events for seminary discussions, nor were they to be lifeless exercises of tradition and routine. They were given with the specific intent of being lived out, understood, and greatly anticipated by all people of God.[9]

The Exodus

ALLEGORICAL INTERPRETATIONS

Before we plunge into the spiritual picture that these *moadim* paint, let us look at some typology used throughout this *Haggadah*. These helpful allegorical interpretations allow us to relate to the Exodus account in a more personal manner and help us to see how the redemptive act of the Messiah is foreshadowed by the Exodus account.

- Egypt = The World System
- Red Sea = The *Mikvah* (baptism)
- Pharaoh = The Adversary
- Moses = Messiah
- Slavery = Bondage to Sin
- Lamb or Blood = Yeshua's Death Sacrifice
- Wilderness = Time of Purging, Testing, Growth
- Leaven = Sin

The greatest imagery created in the Exodus account is that of salvation. In my opinion, the Exodus account is the most powerful picture of how God saves mankind in the whole of our Scriptures. We see throughout this account that God's salvation has always been a demonstration of His mercy, love, and grace. Punctuating this, we read at the conclusion of the book of Exodus:

> Then the LORD passed by in front of him and proclaimed, "The LORD, the LORD God, compassionate and gracious, slow to anger, and abounding in lovingkindness and truth; who keeps lovingkindness for thousands, who forgives iniquity, transgression and sin; yet He will by no means leave the guilty unpunished, visiting the iniquity of fathers on the children and on the grandchildren to the third and fourth generations." Moses made haste to bow low toward

the earth and worship. He said, "If now I have found favor in Your sight, O Lord, I pray, let the Lord go along in our midst, even though the people are so obstinate, and pardon our iniquity and our sin, and take us as Your own possession." (Exodus 34:6–9)

From this passage (verses 6–7) the rabbis have derived the 13 principles of God's mercy. Verse 9, in my opinion, represents a prayer of repentance and salvation. In all of our preparations for and participation in the *seder* service, this reality should be at the forefront of our minds. God saves His people. This is the single most important message and image of the Exodus account.

Cycle of Sanctification

God has a plan. His appointments are purposeful and unique—they work together within the context of one biblical year, throughout our lifetime. All the Feasts listed in Leviticus 23 which are reviewed here, are called *moadim* (singular: *moed*). A *moed* is a unique and significant appointment or meeting between God and man. The *moadim* act as specific teaching tools by causing us to take focused time-outs from our hectic lives in order to experience greater intimacy with our Creator. These times also shadow[10] the Messiah's redemptive work in our lives, which forms the basis for our personal transformation.

Examine the following overview of God's biblical calendar. Look at each feast individually, and look at them as a whole. Upon careful examination, I believe you will begin to see exactly what I mean by the 'cycle of sanctification.'

Shabbat (Sabbath)
A Weekly Practice—Leviticus 23:3

On the *Shabbat* we are commanded by God to cease, rest, rejoice, and worship. We are told not to go our own way or fulfill our own desires, but to rest in the knowledge that God Himself provides for us. The Sabbath is a reminder that we are the Messiah's covenant people—His bride—and He desires for us to experience an intimate time with Him weekly.

The *Shabbat* is also a commemoration of the Exodus from Egypt.[11] The day of rest signifies that we are no longer slaves; only free men can take a day off! The *Shabbat* reminds us that there is no labor that needs to yet be accomplished in order to enter into God's presence. The seventh day is our weekly time of intimacy with the Father—twenty-four uninterrupted hours of freedom from the hectic world. Mostly, the Sabbath teaches us patience and dependence be reminding us who our Provider is. The *Shabbat* is a true gift of grace to man and a demonstration of God's love.

PESACH (PASSOVER)
A MOMENT OF REDEMPTION—LEVITICUS 23:4–5

Pesach is the name of the lamb sacrifice. Our observance of this appointed time marks the anniversary of the atoning sacrifice of our Passover Lamb, Yeshua. The sacrifice offered at Passover during Temple times provides a vivid picture of the necessity of blood in the atonement for sin. It reminds us that mankind cannot come to the Father without this offering from His Son.

Pesach mandates a time for casting out spiritual leaven from our lives. At His last *seder*, Yeshua revealed to the disciples God's ultimate fulfillment of what the service foreshadowed. He explained that He had yet to face the execution stake as John had foretold: "Behold, the Lamb of God who takes away the sin of the world!" (John 1:29).

The *seder* meal (and, if it were possible, the partaking of the *pesach* sacrifice) celebrates our redemption from sin and the bondage we once had to Pharaoh.

> We are free to serve G-d...From slavery, to family, to nation; we experience the presence of our new heightened status and spiritual reality.[12]

The *Pesach seder* service ushers in the entire week of Unleavened Bread—the next feast in the cycle of sanctification.

Chag HaMatzot (Unleavened Bread)
A Time of Abstinence Resulting
in Sanctification—Leviticus 23:6–8

The seven days of Unleavened Bread begin with the *Pesach* meal. By the time the *seder* begins, we are already prepared to cleanse our inner lives and leave Egypt behind. The rituals of the *seder* meal provide specific visual reminders of the burden of sin (Egypt) and the joy of our freedom.

The overarching theme of this specific appointment on God's calendar is sanctification from sin. It is a time for entering a place of freedom to worship God unhindered. This concept is not only recognized by believers today as we study God's Word, but has been taught by rabbis throughout Israel's history. Clearly Paul had this same theme in mind when he used the terms "leaven" and "unleavened" throughout his letters to the community at Corinth.

During the seven days of Unleavened Bread, we are not to eat or possess leaven. The commandment provides a specific and unique physical reality for us today. The physical aspect of this process expresses our inner transformation.

The themes of *Chag HaMatzot* and *Pesach* are so intertwined that their meanings and significance overlap. At *Pesach* we remember the redemption of our lives through the blood of the Lamb, and through the seven days of *Chag HaMatzot*, we experience the removal of all sin (leaven) from our being.

The combination of Passover and the seven days of Unleavened Bread create both physical and spiritual realities in our lives. We experience the freedom from our chains of bondage at Passover, and our walk of faith through the wilderness purifies us from all sin (leaven) that remains in our lives, preparing us to enter the 'Promised Land.' And before the seven days of Unleavened Bread are complete, the countdown to the next appointment on the calendar has already begun.

My family and I have found that the act of fulfilling the commandments related to the spring appointments is most effective when we select one particular sin or area of the flesh to prayerfully bring before God and allow the Master to free us from that bondage. This observance has given my wife and me many opportunities to teach our children on the realities of sin, the process of redemption, and the disciplines of self-control and abstinence.[13]

THE OMER
A SEASON OF MATURATION AND GROWTH—LEVITICUS 23:9–16

The *Omer* is a 49–day countdown to the final spring appointment, Pentecost (*Shavuot*). The *Omer* is an integral link between *Pesach* and *Shavuot*. The days of the *Omer* create a chain between the things we experienced at *Pesach* and *Chag HaMatzot* with *Shavuot*, when we receive a fresh empowering of God's Spirit.

The *Omer* is a time of recognizable growth and maturation. In the land of Israel, it is a period in which the wheat that was planted before Passover is allowed to mature until the time of the harvest 50 days later. The days of the *Omer* also correspond to the days that our Messiah Yeshua walked among His disciples after His resurrection, revealed Himself to hundreds of believers, and ascended to the Father.

SHAVUOT (PENTECOST)
A TIME OF EQUIPPING AND EMPOWERING—LEVITICUS 23:15–21

Seven weeks after *Chag HaMatzot*, the feast of *Shavuot* is the next appointment on the calendar. It is a celebration of God's Spirit revealing His Word. At the first *Shavuot*, the Lord gave the Torah to Moses at Sinai.[14] Fourteen hundred years later, the disciples of the Master were honoring this command and celebrating *Shavuot* at the Temple in Jerusalem when God's Spirit came and empowered them to take the message of the Torah (the ways of the people of God) and the revelation of the Messiah (the way to God) to the Nations.

In our individual lives, *Shavuot* marks the culmination of the greater work that began in us at *Pesach* and followed us through *Chag HaMatzot* and the counting of the *Omer*. Just as the first fruits of the wheat harvest are harvested at *Shavuot*, so too the first fruits of Yeshua's ministry were made evident when the Holy Spirit was poured out on all believers during *Shavuot*.

As believers in Yeshua, the sanctification process of the spring feasts prepares us to receive a new life-giving power that comes only from God's Word (His Torah revealed through the Spirit of Truth that lives within us) and results in us moving ever closer to maturity. Each year, through this process, we are reminded of our covenant relationship to God, our betrothal to Messiah, and our role as believers. *Shavuot* reflects the evidence of our initial fruits of growth. We are now prepared to receive an expanded message of truth and a greater revelation from God.

As the Lord's redeemed people, obeying God's commandments and meeting with our Master during the appointed times provide an opportunity to experience a renewed joy of our salvation. We are equipped again and again, year after year, with a deeper understanding of God's Torah and our salvation in Messiah. Having a fresh empowerment of the Holy Spirit in our lives, we can overcome the areas of significant weakness and sin that previously held us back from being effective witnesses of our Master.[15]

YOM TERUAH (TRUMPETS)
A CALL TO RETURN AND REMEMBER—LEVITICUS 23:23–25

The Feast of Trumpets (traditionally *Rosh HaShanah*) is a day of trumpet blasting and remembrance. After the long, warm, busy summer, we are beckoned back once again to prepare for the sanctification process that God designed in His appointed times. The sound of the ram's horn reminds us that it is a time for settling accounts, repenting, apologizing, forgiving, reconciling, and refocusing on what God is doing in our lives. It is a time to honestly evaluate our progress and determine our shortcomings—those areas where we fell short of the divine revelation given to us at 'Sinai,' *Shavuot.*

Yom Teruah prophetically foreshadows the trumpet that heralds the coming of Messiah, His coronation in Jerusalem, and the ingathering and resurrection of the dead. On the Feast of Trumpets, we repent with an urgency inspired by the coming of the next appointment, just ten days away.

YOM KIPPUR (DAY OF ATONEMENT)
A DAY OF RECKONING—LEVITICUS 23:26–32

Six months after experiencing freedom from our bondage during the spring appointments, we humble our souls by fasting and take an entire day to pour out prayers of confession and contrition. It is a day of cleansing and recommitment, a preparation for the next and final appointment on God's calendar.

The Day of Atonement teaches us the depth of the redemptive work accomplished for us in Yeshua's death at Passover. It teaches us that the atonement, grace, and sufficiency of His sacrifice are ongoing. *Yom Kippur* also leads us to an understanding of Messiah's role as our High Priest.

Yom Kippur is a day of reckoning. It is an annual reminder of the day when our High Priest entered the Holy of Holies to make atonement for our sins. This day also brings to mind John's vision of the Book of Life being opened and all humanity giving account before our Maker.[16]

SUKKOT (TABERNACLES)
CELEBRATING THE COMPLETED WORK—LEVITICUS 23:33–43

The Feast of Tabernacles is a time of great rejoicing; it is a commemoration of our time in the wilderness and our anticipation of the Messianic era to come. During *Sukkot,* we celebrate the abundant harvest and rejoice in the work that God has done in our lives. The cycle is now complete, and sanctification gives way to sheer, unfettered joy. We are commanded to rejoice at the Feast of Tabernacles. Together, we celebrate and enjoy the abundance of God's provision. We enjoy the Kingdom of Heaven on earth as we look forward to that coming reality.

We camp out in a booth (*sukkah*) to celebrate the fact that God dwelt with man both in the desert and in the person of Messiah Yeshua, and we anticipate God's final dwelling with us here on earth in Jerusalem.

Summary

Also in the day of your gladness and in your appointed feasts, and on the first days of your months, you shall blow the trumpets over your burnt offerings and over the sacrifices of your peace offerings; and they will be a memorial for you before your God: I am the Lord your God. (Numbers 10:10)

Another way that the Torah refers to the *moadim* is by calling them "the day of your gladness" or *yom simchat'chem* (יוֹם שִׂמְחַתְכֶם). Surely, the people of God are meant to experience great joy with one another and with God on these unique days to which He has called us to meet Him.

In the same way that God causes new fruit and new life to come forth through the changing of His seasons, He also renews His creation. Through His *moadim*, a 'cycle of sanctification' is formed through which new fruit and greater life can come forth from His people. His kingdom is full of order and in that kingdom there is life—His life—and it produces joy and contentment within us as the people of God!

Our participation is a critical element needed to encounter our Maker at His appointed times. These days are neither random theological exercises nor mere thoughts in our minds. God uses these holy days to free us from bondage and transform us into the image of Messiah. His feasts are tools in our lives that daily and annually mature us, heal us, and sanctify us.

In summary, participation in the appointed time each year creates a constant process of maturation. Why? Because the feasts of the Lord are tools that the Father uses to shape us as His holy people. Consider the following "C's" as an overview of this process:

- ↜ SHABBAT (Ceasing): We rest our hearts, minds and bodies. This weekly discipline enables us to learn how to effectively put aside the cares of the world in order to train ourselves to focus on matters of the Spirit.

- ↜ PASSOVER (Conception): Something new is birthed within us. We are delivered from old bondage and learn to take our first baby steps into newness of life by abstaining from our old, fleshly nature during the seven days of Unleavened Bread.

- OMER (Connecting): We make practical steps toward overcoming sin. Counting the 50 days following Passover links the work of redemption that took place at *Pesach* to the empowering work of the Spirit in our lives through His Word at Shavuot.

- SHAVUOT (Celebration): We rejoice in God's finished work! We utilize the new ability we gained through the Omer in saying "No!" to sin so that we are ready to run at *Shavuot*—ready to run in strength and steadfastness in following the leading of the Spirit of the Lord. The old sin of our lives has been left behind, and we experience a renewed sense of the joy of our salvation.

- YOM TERUAH (Call): We pay attention and prepare for God's atonement. The Holy Day of "Blowing" heralds the people of God to ready ourselves and our hearts for the greatest and most solemn day on the biblical calendar—Yom Kippur.

- YOM KIPPUR (Consummation): God consummates what He started at *Pesach*. We realize the new fullness of our lives after having gone through a process of crucifying our flesh. This is also a time of reassurance that our sins (past and future) are forgiven and have been fully atoned for.

- SUKKOT (Conclusion): We celebrate the completed work. The harvest is plentiful and we rejoice as we acknowledge and realize the growth we have made in our spiritual lives. We look toward the upcoming cycle and yearn for Messiah to tabernacle with us in a deeper and fuller way.

Not Your Typical Haggadah

This Passover *Haggadah* is written with specific intent. It emphasizes the practical redemption from sin in the lives of the redeemed. It forces the participants to examine and consider their lives in the light of being called out and set free. Therefore, while I appreciate the beauty of tradition, I have altered the traditional *seder* slightly to enable the participant to focus on the thrust of this particular *Haggadah*.

In creating this contemporary approach to honoring Passover, we know that we do not function in a vacuum. While we did depart from ancient practices in certain parts of this *Haggadah*, we still felt responsible to observe this *moed* in the way it has been celebrated for thousands of years.

Moreover, I try to balance creativity with the desire to conserve and adapt what speaks to us from the past.[17] This service is structured to allow the feast to impact our lives, enabling us all to encounter Passover.

The spiritual nature of this ritual will allow us to corporately and individually mark *Pesach* as a specific moment on God's ongoing annual calendar, in which we each personally experience a renewed sense of our deliverance. As we once again turn away from and leave behind the slavery we experience when we live in 'Egypt,' we will begin to sing a new song of joy and freedom because of the work that is being done in our lives at this time.

This *Haggadah* is meant to encourage us to live in a sanctified and separate manner. To put it another way, our outer lives should be a direct reflection of our inner changes.

As a sanctified people, we cannot accept sin. The Torah demands our separation from it. It calls for holiness. The Scriptures require a people set free from bondage, a people who respond righteously to God by living holy, sanctified lives. God, in His infinite wisdom, recognized that we need assistance in living out this transformation. When we submit our lives, both corporately and individually, to the work of God through obedience to His *moadim,* the appointed times become the means through which God facilitates a natural, rhythmic healing and restoration process in our lives.

Each year the Father desires to bring us through the sea and into new levels of freedom from sin. Our Master not only redeems—He equips. It is my prayer that this approach to God's *moadim* will transform you in ways you have never before experienced.

Seder Fundamentals
Why Is this Night Different?

In Jewish tradition, the saga of God's miraculous redemption of Israel from Egypt during the first Passover is eloquently evoked in one simple question: "Why is this night different from all other nights?"

To answer this question, we refer to our ancestors. We recall their bondage. We relate to their struggles, their fear, their redemption, and their freedom. We are reminded of the work of the Lord both historically and personally, and we rejoice in the work that God has done on our behalf as His people.

> You shall fear the LORD your God; you shall serve Him and cling to Him, and you shall swear by His name. He is your praise and He is your God, Who has done these great and awesome things for you which your eyes have seen. (Deuteronomy 10:20–21)

Our winters are hard and arduous times that challenge each of us. Through the cold and bitter storms that come, we have much time to labor, search our souls, and reflect. Yet we see our deliverance coming and we eagerly wait for our intimate meeting with our Maker once again.

How Do I Tell the Story?

As a memorial[18] of the *pesach*, we conduct a *seder* to fulfill the biblical command to tell our children how the Lord delivered Israel from Egypt. The *seder* is a structured order that enables participants to enter into a personal encounter with history and with the Lord. It is also a wonderfully crafted educational tool, inviting questions and commentary from all who participate.

You shall tell your son on that day, saying, "It is because of what the LORD did for me when I came out of Egypt." (Exodus 13:8)

Traditionally the *seder* is told by reading through a *Haggadah* like this one. The Hebrew word *Haggadah* means "the telling." Through illustrations, aromas, tastes, and songs, we recall the history of our people and the wonderful works of our God. Experiencing these traditional elements is an important part of our connection to the land and people of greater Israel.

The purpose of the traditional *seder* is to bring the story of redemption to those at the table so that each one feels as if he were experiencing God's redemption for the first time.

I believe that one of the greatest traditions of the Jewish people is the tradition of innovation. Throughout history, Jewish people have been innovative in the way they adapt to the culture, time, and place in which they have been planted. I have developed this *Haggadah* with the same 'tradition of innovation' in mind.

I feel that such a focused approach to Passover will enable God's timeless truths to have a greater impact on the personal lives of believers everywhere. Thus, my goal is to focus on the continued process of sanctification available to believers who chose to walk according to God's ways while stepping back from time, traditions,[19] and some extrabiblical influences in order to place our emphasis on two major themes.

First, we will recall the events leading to Israel's exodus by reading through the biblical description of the account. This telling will be punctuated by a series of questions posed by children to participants in the *seder* and a powerful reading of the Ten Words in Exodus 20.

Second, we will focus on the redemptive nature of this day in our own personal lives. These truths will be emphasized through partaking of the biblically mandated *matzah* and bitter herbs as well as the traditional four cups. Through this approach, I hope that we will tap into the essential spiritual quality of this appointment.

WHAT ABOUT THE FOUR CUPS OF WINE?

The Scripture from which traditional Judaism has derived the four cups[20] of wine at a Passover *seder* is drawn from is Exodus 6:6–7, which states:

> Say, therefore, to the sons of Israel,

- ❧ "I am the LORD, and I will bring you out from under the burdens of the Egyptians," (Cup of Sanctification)
- ❧ "and I will deliver you from their bondage," (Cup of Deliverance)
- ❧ "and I will also redeem you with an outstretched arm and with great judgments," (Cup of Redemption)
- ❧ "and I will take you for My people, and I will be your God; and you shall know that I am the LORD your God, who brought you out from under the burdens of the Egyptians." (Cup of Hope)

These four cups have structured *Haggadot* through the ages and likewise help structure this *Haggadah* to form significant transitional points within this *seder*. Since they play a critical role in our ceremony, let's spend some time analyzing each cup.

THE CUP OF SANCTIFICATION

"Let my people go from under the burdens of the Egyptians so that they may serve Me." The Lord desired to set His people apart in order that they might enter into a process of sanctification with Him and learn to worship God as He desired. Through their sanctification process, the Israelites learned what holiness, purity, and consecration to their new Master meant.

THE CUP OF DELIVERANCE

"I will deliver you from your bondage." God promised to deliver His people from bondage so that they could worship Him freely. In so doing, Adonai was making a statement about the gods of this world and their weakness in comparison to His ultimate rescue.

THE CUP OF REDEMPTION

"I will redeem you with a mighty hand and an outstretched arm." This cup acknowledges that the work of redemption is a work of God alone. It is He alone who can ransom His people back to Himself and recover them from the grip of Egypt.

THE CUP OF HOPE

"I will take you for My people and I will be your God." Adonai graciously gave His children the trust and confidence of a future plan for their relationship with him. This cup is drunk in connection to Elijah and the coming of Messiah. We can relate to the expectations of our Israelite ancestors when we drink this cup in that we believe the Lord will complete His promises to send the Messiah, bringing peace to our world.

BIBLICALLY BASED OBJECTIVES OF THE SEDER

The Passover *seder* is more than just a unique dinner experience with friends and family. It is more than simply an opportunity for outreach.[21] The Passover *seder* begins a cycle that illuminates the greatest redemptive work known to man. The *seder* contained in this *Haggadah* is an invention of man that holds the following biblically based spiritual objectives:

1. Relate the story of the events leading to the redemption of Israel to our children as a fulfillment of the Torah's command to do so. (See Exodus 13:8.)

2. Teach our children and remind ourselves that it was the sole intervention of God that brought about the redemption of mankind, and to do so through the use

of all our senses (i.e., smell, touch, taste, see, hear) as well as through the spoken word, music, and worship. (See Exodus 10:2; Deuteronomy 7:19.)

3. Recount the wondrous miracles God performed in Egypt as evidence of His intervention in the lives of those He loves. (See Exodus 10:2; 13:14; Deuteronomy 4:34; 10:21.)

4. Recall the miraculous escape of Israel from the plagues that had smitten the Egyptians as further evidence of God's intervention in the lives of His chosen. (See Exodus 12:13, 14, 23, 24; Deuteronomy 7:22, 23.)

5. Remember that God's intervention was the result of His mercy and unwarranted love and grace. Also, we recall that our God is a God of covenantal faithfulness. (See Deuteronomy 4:37; 7:8; Exodus 13:8.)

6. Realize that the account of the Exodus is an everlasting assurance that the Almighty will smite all enemies of His people, provided those people walk in His protective guards (commandments), listening to and responding to His voice (His Word). (See Deuteronomy 28–29; Proverbs 19:16.)

7. Appreciate one's status and position in God's family by recalling the bondage and condition of Israel prior to her redemption. By personally relating to this historical bondage, slavery, and burden, we hope to call to mind the work that God performed in order to free us from slavery to sin and death. (See Deuteronomy 5:15; 6:10–15; Psalm 51:13–15.)

8. Build on the analogy Paul taught the Corinthians regarding Passover, Unleavened Bread, and abstinence from sin. (See 1 Corinthians 5:6–8.)

The Seder

SANCTIFICATION

DELIVERANCE

REDEMPTION

HOPE

IF THE *SEDER* FALLS ON FRIDAY NIGHT, BEGIN HERE. [22]

HOST As we begin this designated time for the Lord, this year we also begin the seventh day of the week, the *Shabbat*.

וַיְהִי עֶרֶב, וַיְהִי בֹקֶר	*Vay'hi erev, vay'hi voker*
יוֹם הַשִּׁשִּׁי	*Yom hashishi*
וַיְכֻלּוּ הַשָּׁמַיִם	*Vay'chulu hashamayim*
וְהָאָרֶץ וְכָל־צְבָאָם,	*v'ha-aretz v'chol tz'va-am,*
וַיְכַל אֱלֹהִים	*vay'chal Elohim*
בַּיּוֹם הַשְּׁבִיעִי	*bayom hash'vi-i*
מְלַאכְתּוֹ אֲשֶׁר עָשָׂה;	*m'lach'to asher asa;*
וַיִּשְׁבֹּת בַּיּוֹם הַשְּׁבִיעִי	*vayish'bot bayom hash'vi-i*
מִכָּל־מְלַאכְתּוֹ אֲשֶׁר עָשָׂה.	*mikol m'lach'to asher asa.*
וַיְבָרֶךְ אֱלֹהִים	*Vay'varech Elohim*
אֶת יוֹם הַשְּׁבִיעִי	*et yom hash'vi-i*
וַיְקַדֵּשׁ אֹתוֹ,	*vay'kadeish oto,*
כִּי בוֹ שָׁבַת מִכָּל־מְלַאכְתּוֹ	*ki vo shavat mikol m'lach'to*
אֲשֶׁר־בָּרָא אֱלֹהִים לַעֲשׂוֹת.	*asher bara Elohim la'asot.*

ALL And there was evening and there was morning, the sixth day. Thus the heavens and the earth were completed, and all their hosts. By the seventh day God completed His work which He had done, and He rested on the seventh day from all His work which He had done. Then God blessed the seventh day and sanctified it, because in it He rested from all His work which God had created and made.

HOST The Lord commands us to:

Remember the Sabbath day, to keep it holy. Six days you shall labor and do all your work, but the seventh day is a Sabbath of the LORD your God; in it you shall not do any work...For in six days the LORD made the heavens and the earth, the sea and all that is in them, and rested on the seventh day; therefore the LORD blessed the Sabbath day and made it holy. (Exodus 20:8–11)

ON ALL OTHER NIGHTS, BEGIN HERE.
ON FRIDAY NIGHT, WORDS IN BRACKETS ARE INCLUDED.

בָּרוּךְ אַתָּה יהוה	Baruch ata Adonai
אֱלֹהֵינוּ מֶלֶךְ הָעוֹלָם	Eloheinu Melech ha-olam
אֲשֶׁר בָּחַר בָּנוּ מִכָּל עָם	asher bachar banu mikol am
וְרוֹמְמָנוּ מִכָּל לָשׁוֹן	v'rom'manu mikol lashon
וְקִדְּשָׁנוּ בְּמִצְוֹתָיו.	vikid'shanu b'mitz'votav.
וַתִּתֶּן לָנוּ יהוה אֱלֹהֵינוּ,	V'titen lanu Adonai Eloheinu,
בְּאַהֲבָה (שַׁבָּתוֹת לִמְנוּחָה וּ)	b'ahavah (shabbatot lim'nucha u)
מוֹעֲדִים לְשִׂמְחָה חַגִּים	mo'adim l'sim'cha chagim
וּזְמַנִּים לְשָׂשׂוֹן אֶת יוֹם	uz'manim l'sason et yom
(הַשַּׁבָּת הַזֶּה וְאֶת יוֹם)	(hashabbat hazeh v'et yom)
חַג הַמַּצּוֹת הַזֶּה	chag hamatzot hazeh
זְמַן חֵרוּתֵנוּ (בְּאַהֲבָה)	z'man cheiruteinu (b'ahavah)
מִקְרָא קֹדֶשׁ,	mik'ra kodesh,
זֵכֶר לִיצִיאַת מִצְרַיִם,	zeicher litziat mitz'raim,
כִּי בָנוּ בָחַרְתָּ	ki vanu vachar'ta
וְאוֹתָנוּ קִדַּשְׁתָּ	v'otanu kidashta,
מִכָּל הָעַמִּים (וְשַׁבָּת)	mikol ha'amim (v'shabbat)
וּמוֹעֲדֵי קָדְשְׁךָ	u'mo'adei kad'shecha
(בְּאַהֲבָה וּבְרָצוֹן) בְּשִׂמְחָה	(b'ahavah uv'ratzon) b'sim'cha
וּבְשָׂשׂוֹן הִנְחַלְתָּנוּ.	uv'sasson hin'chal'tanu.
בָּרוּךְ אַתָּה יהוה	Baruch ata Adonai
מְקַדֵּשׁ (הַשַּׁבָּת וּ)	m'kadeish (hashabbat u)
יִשְׂרָאֵל וְהַזְּמַנִּים.	Yisrael v'haz'manim.

ALL Blessed are you, Lord our God, King of the universe, Who has chosen us from every people, exalted us above every tongue, and sanctified us with His commandments. And You gave us, Lord our God, with love (Sabbaths for rest), appointed festivals for gladness, festivals and times for joy,

(this day of Sabbath and) this day of the Feast of Unleavened Bread, the time of our freedom (with love) a holy convocation, a memorial of the Exodus from Egypt. For You have chosen us and You have sanctified us above all the peoples, (and the Sabbath) and Your holy festivals (in love and in favor) in gladness and in joy have You granted us as a heritage. Blessed are you, Lord our God, Who sanctifies (the Sabbath and) Israel and the seasons.

ON SATURDAY NIGHT ADD: [23]

HOST

בָּרוּךְ אַתָּה יהוה   *Baruch ata Adonai*
אֱלֹהֵינוּ מֶלֶךְ הָעוֹלָם,   *Eloheinu Melech ha-olam,*
בּוֹרֵא מְאוֹרֵי הָאֵשׁ.   *borei m'ohrei ha-esh.*

בָּרוּךְ אַתָּה יהוה   *Baruch ata Adonai*
אֱלֹהֵינוּ מֶלֶךְ הָעוֹלָם,   *Eloheinu Melech ha-olam,*
הַמַּבְדִּיל בֵּין קֹדֶשׁ לְחוֹל,   *hamav'dil bein kodesh l'chol*
בֵּין אוֹר לְחֹשֶׁךְ,   *bein ohr l'choshech*
בֵּין יִשְׂרָאֵל לָעַמִּים,   *bein Yisrael la'amim,*
בֵּין יוֹם הַשְּׁבִיעִי   *bein yom hash'vi-i*
לְשֵׁשֶׁת יְמֵי הַמַּעֲשֶׂה,   *l'sheshet y'mei hama'aseh,*
בֵּין קְדֻשַּׁת שַׁבָּת   *bein k'dushat shabbat,*
לִקְדֻשַּׁת יוֹם טוֹב הִבְדַּלְתָּ,   *lik'dushat yom tov hiv'dal'ta,*
וְאֶת יוֹם הַשְּׁבִיעִי מִשֵּׁשֶׁת   *v'et yom hash'vi-i misheshet*
יְמֵי הַמַּעֲשֶׂה קִדַּשְׁתָּ,   *y'mei hama'ase kidash'ta,*
הִבְדַּלְתָּ וְקִדַּשְׁתָּ   *hiv'dal'ta v'kidash'ta*
אֶת עַמְּךָ יִשְׂרָאֵל   *et am'cha Yisrael*
בִּקְדֻשָּׁתֶךָ.   *bik'dushatecha.*
בָּרוּךְ אַתָּה יהוה   *Baruch ata Adonai*
הַמַּבְדִּיל בֵּין קֹדֶשׁ לְקֹדֶשׁ.   *hamav'dil bein kodesh l'kodesh.*

Blessed are You, Lord our God, King of the universe, Who creates the illumination of the fire.

Blessed are You, Lord our God, King of the universe, Who separates between holy and secular, between light and darkness, between Israel and the nations, between the seventh day and the six days of labor. You made a distinction between the holiness of the Sabbath and the holiness of the festivals, separated the seventh day from the six days of labor, separated and sanctified Your people Israel with Your holiness. Blessed are You, Lord our God, Who made a distinction between holy and holy.

ON ALL OTHER NIGHTS, CONTINUE HERE:

HOST   You shall take a bunch of hyssop and dip it in the blood which is in the basin, and apply some of the blood that is in the basin to the lintel and the two doorposts; and none of you shall go outside the door of his house until morning. For the LORD will pass through to smite the Egyptians; and when He sees the blood on the lintel and on the two doorposts, the LORD will pass over the door and will not allow the destroyer to come in to your houses to smite you. And you shall observe this event as an ordinance for you and your children forever. (Exodus 12:22–24)

When you enter the land which the LORD will give you, as He has promised, you shall observe this rite. And when your children say to you, "What does this rite mean to you?" you shall say, "It is a Passover sacrifice to the LORD who passed over the houses of the sons of Israel in Egypt when He smote the Egyptians, but spared our homes." And the people bowed low and worshiped. Then the sons of Israel went and did so; just as the LORD had commanded Moses and Aaron, so they did. (Exodus 12:25–28)

Generation after generation, the Lord meets with us at this moment; it is a time of transition.[24] As the sun descends and day turns to night, so do we cross over from the old ways of bondage to a new life of freedom. Let us ready our hearts for the Lord's *Pesach*, "for Messiah our Passover also has been sacrificed" (1 Corinthians 5:7). Let us bless Adonai, King of the universe, Who has kept us in life, and sustained us, and enabled us to reach this season.

27

Thankful for coming to this time and season, we pray.

בָּרוּךְ אַתָּה יהוה   *Baruch ata Adonai*
אֱלֹהֵינוּ מֶלֶךְ הָעוֹלָם,   *Eloheinu Melech ha-olam,*
שֶׁהֶחֱיָנוּ וְקִיְּמָנוּ   *shehecheyanu v'kiyemanu*
וְהִגִּיעָנוּ לַזְּמַן הַזֶּה.   *v'higianu laz'man hazeh.*

ALL Blessed are You, Lord our God, King of the universe, Who has kept us in life, and sustained us, and enabled us to reach this festive season.

HOST With the mighty work of God on behalf of the Israelites before us, we now ask the Father not only to recall His mighty work to our minds, but to allow us to encounter it ourselves. We will identify with this redemptive work and cry out personally to God to redeem us from the bondage of our flesh and sinful habit patterns that separate us from His presence.

> It is a night to be observed for the LORD for having brought them out from the land of Egypt; this night is for the LORD, to be observed by all the sons of Israel throughout their generations. (Exodus 12:42)

Throughout this evening let us be vigilant to closely examine our lives and look honestly at our hearts. Are there areas of repetitive sin or fleshly habit patterns in our lives? Do we see a particular sin or area of flesh causing great pain to others? Are there ungodly thought patterns or unrighteous relationships in our lives? Have we become sick and tired of a sin or an area of flesh that we cannot seem to conquer?

This evening we will be reminded of the work of the Lord, both historically and personally, and we will rejoice in the work that He has done on our behalf. This is an appointment of God, and we will once again experience His redemption. He will set us free and sanctify us among all peoples.

You shall fear the LORD your God; you shall serve Him and cling to Him, and you shall swear by His name. He is your praise and He is your God, Who has done these great and awesome things for you which your eyes have seen. (Deuteronomy 10:20–21)

HOST Our Redeemer, the Messiah Yeshua, commanded that when we participate in the Passover *seder* we do it in remembrance of Him. In the days following Yeshua's last *Pesach*, God did a mighty act of redemption. He made redemption available to all mankind. With great compassion God sent His Son to die on our behalf. His redemptive work has set us free from the laws of sin and death that have bound and hindered us from worshiping Him unimpeded.[25]

Then came the first day of Unleavened Bread on which the Passover lamb had to be sacrificed. And Yeshua sent Peter and John, saying, "Go and prepare the Passover for us, so that we may eat it."

They said to Him, "Where do You want us to prepare it?"

And He said to them, "When you have entered the city, a man will meet you carrying a pitcher of water; follow him into the house that he enters. And you shall say to the owner of the house, 'The Teacher says to you, "Where is the guest room in which I may eat the Passover with My disciples?"' And he will show you a large, furnished upper room; prepare it there."

And they left and found everything just as He had told them; and they prepared the Passover.

When the hour had come, He reclined at the table, and the apostles with Him. And He said to them, "I have earnestly desired to eat this *Pesach* with you before I suffer; for I say to you, I shall never again eat it until it is fulfilled in the kingdom of God." And when He had taken a cup and given thanks, He said, "Take this and share it among yourselves; for I say to you, I will not drink of the fruit of the vine from

now on until the kingdom of God comes." And when He had taken some bread and given thanks, He broke it and gave it to them, saying, "This is My body which is given for you; do this in remembrance of Me." And in the same way He took the cup after they had eaten, saying, "This cup which is poured out for you is the new covenant in My blood." [26] (Luke 22:7–20)

HOST Our true freedom from sin and our right standing before God was accomplished by His servant Yeshua. It is through our total acceptance and faith in the death, burial, and resurrection of the Messiah Yeshua that we find life. We now identify with that work once again.

The First Cup

Sanctification

וְהוֹצֵאתִי

"I am the LORD, and I will
bring you out from under the
burdens of the Egyptians."

TAKE THE FIRST CUP AND SAY:

HOST

בָּרוּךְ אַתָּה יהוה
אֱלֹהֵינוּ מֶלֶךְ הָעוֹלָם,
בּוֹרֵא פְּרִי הַגָּפֶן.

*Baruch ata Adonai
Eloheinu Melech ha-olam,
borei p'ri hagafen.*

ALL Blessed are You, Lord our God, King of the universe, Who creates the fruit of the vine.

DRINK THE FIRST CUP

HOST The first cup marks Israel as God's chosen[27]—as the people for whom He would bring deliverance from under the burden of slavery, freeing them to worship and serve Him in spirit and in truth. This is the same work He does for each and every child He brings into His family.[28] He chooses them of His own sovereign will and sets about to free them from the shackles of slavery. This freedom is for one purpose: to serve Him as He intends. It is the calling of each and every child of God to be sanctified—set apart unto God, to be given over to His service and His service alone. The first cup of the *seder,* the cup of sanctification or separation, reminds us of this crucial starting point of our salvation.

Lord, You have sanctified us; You have called us to "be holy as you are Holy."[29] We thank You, *Abba,* that You have allowed us to rediscover Your holy Torah, enabling us to grasp the fullness of Scripture, without which fullness of life in the Messiah Yeshua cannot be fully realized. You have preserved for Yourself a remnant people and called us to be a light and the salt of the earth.

READER You are the salt of the earth; but if the salt has become tasteless, how can it be made salty again? It is no longer good for anything, except to be thrown out and trampled under foot by men. You are the light of the world. A city set on a hill cannot be hidden; nor does anyone light a lamp and put it under a basket, but on the lampstand, and it gives light to all who are in the house. Let your light shine before men in such a way that they may see your good works, and glorify your Father who is in heaven. (Matthew 5:13–16)

HOST May we be a people who carry Your Name and declare Your praise. Contemplate the words of this song. May they set the stage for this evening.

SONG

SONG #1 : THE PESACH SONG (WE'RE LEAVING) : PG. 92
OR
SONG #4 : YOU HAVE CALLED ME : PG. 95

THE FOUR QUESTIONS

CHILD Why are we to select a lamb from the flock and set it apart from the others?

ADULT It is to be the Lord's *Pesach*. He has seen our need and prepared in advance His perfect sacrifice for us.

CHILD Why is the Lord's *Pesach* to be sacrificed on this night?

ADULT It was on this night many generations ago that ADONAI set our people free from the anguish and oppression of slavery. We are to eat the *Pesach* tonight because this is what our fathers ate the night they were set free.

CHILD Why did our forefathers spread the blood of the *Pesach* on the door frames of their homes? What is meant by this ceremony?

ADULT The Lord commanded our fathers to mark their homes with the blood of the lamb to serve as a sign, so that as He passed through Egypt to kill the Egyptians He would pass over and not strike them. It is the sacrifice of the Lord's *Pesach* because the Lord our God passed over the houses of the people of Israel in Egypt when He struck down the Egyptians, and spared the homes of our ancestors.

WITHOUT THE TEMPLE THE FOLLOWING QUESTION IS ASKED.

CHILD Why do we not slaughter the lamb today?

ADULT The Lord has commanded us to sacrifice the *Pesach* in the place where He will choose to have His name live.[30] We wait for the day when our Messiah returns and reestablishes His government and the Temple. Then we will be able to keep this rite in God's holy city, Jerusalem. Until that day, we eat the *matzah* and the bitter herbs, and we tell the story of the Exodus.

THE SETTING

HOST The Torah reveals to us a God who works directly in the lives of His people. He is a covenant-faithful God who promises, guides, sets apart, and gives freedom to His chosen ones. The children of Israel were unable to serve the Lord; they were in bondage to a cruel system that held them captive. They were oppressed, tired, and weak, but God brought them their freedom. Throughout this telling, we will continually hear the appeal, "Let My people go," followed by the passionate, inviting statement "that they may serve Me." This is the story of a God whose goal is to sanctify, deliver, and redeem His people.

Before Moses, there was Abraham, with whom the Lord made a covenant and foretold of the troubling times ahead.

READER God said to Abram, "Know for certain that your descendants will be strangers in a land that is not theirs, where they will be enslaved and oppressed four hundred years. But I will also judge the nation whom they will serve, and afterward they will come out with many possessions." (Genesis 15:13–14)

HOST That foreign land was Egypt, and Israel was forced there by famine in the land of Canaan. It was through Joseph—Abraham's great-grandson—that the Lord protected and provided for all of Israel.

READER [The brothers of Joseph] said to Pharaoh, "We have come to sojourn in the land, for there is no pasture for your servants' flocks, for the famine is severe in the land of Canaan. Now, therefore, please let your servants live in the land of Goshen."

Then Pharaoh said to Joseph, "Your father and your brothers have come to you. The land of Egypt is at your disposal; settle your father and your brothers in the best of the land, let them live in the land of Goshen; and if you know any capable men among them, then put them in charge of my livestock." (Genesis 47:4–6)

HOST Then one day, a new king arose over Egypt—one who did not know Joseph and his brothers.

READER [This new king] said to his people, "Behold, the people of the sons of Israel are more and mightier than we. Come, let us deal wisely with them, or else they will multiply and in the event of war, they will also join themselves to those who hate us, and fight against us and depart from the land." So they appointed taskmasters over them to afflict them with hard labor…But the more they afflicted them, the more they multiplied and the more they spread out, so that they were in dread of the sons of Israel. (Exodus 1:9–12)

HOST Pharaoh appointed taskmasters over God's people and…

ALL …afflicted them (Exodus 1:11)

forced hard labor upon them (Exodus 1:14)

abused them (Exodus 1:14)

made them labor rigorously (Exodus 1:14)

killed their children (Exodus 1:22)

 THE BITTER HERBS (MAROR)

HOST Why do we eat this bitter herb?[31] It is to remind us that the Egyptians embittered the lives of our fathers in Egypt, as it is written:

> They made their lives bitter with hard labor in mortar and bricks and at all kinds of labor in the field, all their labors which they rigorously imposed on them. (Exodus 1:14)

Let us now identify with the bitterness, the pain, and the suffering of our ancestors and eat, as commanded, the bitter herb.

HOST

בָּרוּךְ אַתָּה יהוה *Baruch ata Adonai*
אֱלֹהֵינוּ מֶלֶךְ הָעוֹלָם, *Eloheinu Melech ha-olam,*
אֲשֶׁר קִדְּשָׁנוּ בְּמִצְוֹתָיו *asher kid'shanu b'mitz'votav*
וְצִוָּנוּ עַל אֲכִילַת מָרוֹר. *v'tzivanu al achilat maror.*

ALL Blessed are You, Lord our God, King of the universe, Who has sanctified us with Your commandsments, and commanded us to eat bitter herbs.

As we take the *maror*, let us eat and remember.

TRY NOT TO DRINK AFTER THE PARTAKING OF THE *MAROR*.
IF POSSIBLE, ALLOW THE TASTE AND STING TO LINGER IN YOUR MOUTH.

 THE CALL—GOD HEARD THEIR CRY

HOST The Lord's plan was clear—He would use a people to make His Name known throughout the world. Despite times of trouble, apparent separation, and questioning, the Lord was ever present.

READER Now it came about in the course of those many days that the king of Egypt died. And the sons of Israel sighed because of the bondage, and they cried out; and their cry for help because of their bondage rose up to God. So God heard their groaning; and God remembered His covenant with Abraham, Isaac, and Jacob. God saw the sons of Israel, and God took notice of them. (Exodus 2:23–25)

HOST   Remembering His covenant with Abraham, God set in motion a plan to remove His chosen ones from their oppression.

READER   The LORD said, "I have surely seen the affliction of My people who are in Egypt, and have given heed to their cry because of their taskmasters, for I am aware of their sufferings. So I have come down to deliver them from the power of the Egyptians, and to bring them up from that land to a good and spacious land, to a land flowing with milk and honey...Now, behold, the cry of the sons of Israel has come to Me; furthermore, I have seen the oppression with which the Egyptians are oppressing them." (Exodus 3:7–9)

READER   ...the LORD, the God of your fathers, the God of Abraham, Isaac and Jacob, has appeared to me, saying, "I am indeed concerned about you and what has been done to you in Egypt." (Exodus 3:16)

HOST   God used Moses, set apart at birth, to deliver His message to the elders of Israel and ultimately to Pharaoh. After much debate, doubt, and fear, Moses gathered together Aaron and the elders of Israel and revealed to them God's plan. For it is said:

READER   Now the LORD said to Aaron, "Go to meet Moses in the wilderness." So he went and met him at the mountain of God and kissed him. Moses told Aaron all the words of the LORD with which He had sent him, and all the signs that He had commanded him to do. Then Moses and Aaron went and assembled all the elders of the sons of Israel; and Aaron spoke all the words which the LORD had spoken to Moses. He then performed the signs in the sight of the people. So the people believed; and when they heard that

the LORD was concerned about the sons of Israel and that He had seen their affliction, then they bowed low and worshiped. (Exodus 4:27–31)

✿ THE DELIVERANCE ✿

HOST Despite great insecurity, fear, and trepidation, Moses went to Pharaoh to communicate God's plan. Pharaoh mocked, resisted and discounted the Lord's ability to save His people.

READER Again Pharaoh said, "Look, the people of the land are now many, and you would have them cease from their labors!" So the same day Pharaoh commanded the taskmasters over the people and their foremen, saying, "You are no longer to give the people straw to make brick as previously; let them go and gather straw for themselves. But the quota of bricks which they were making previously, you shall impose on them; you are not to reduce any of it. Because they are lazy, therefore they cry out, 'Let us go and sacrifice to our God.' Let the labor be heavier on the men, and let them work at it so that they will pay no attention to false words." So the taskmasters of the people and their foremen went out and spoke to the people, saying, "Thus says Pharaoh, 'I am not going to give you any straw.'" (Exodus 5:5–10)

HOST Let us again eat the *maror* as we remember how Pharaoh increased Israel's bitter conditions to break their spirit.

HOST

בָּרוּךְ אַתָּה יהוה   *Baruch ata Adonai*
אֱלֹהֵינוּ מֶלֶךְ הָעוֹלָם,   *Eloheinu Melech ha-olam,*
אֲשֶׁר קִדְּשָׁנוּ בְּמִצְוֹתָיו   *asher kid'shanu b'mitz'votav*
וְצִוָּנוּ עַל אֲכִילַת מָרוֹר.   *v'tzivanu al achilat maror.*

ALL Blessed are You, Lord our God, King of the universe, Who has sanctified us with Your commandments, and commanded us to eat bitter herbs.

As we take the *maror*, let us eat and remember.

TRY NOT TO DRINK AFTER THE PARTAKING OF THE *MAROR*.
IF POSSIBLE, ALLOW THE TASTE AND STING TO LINGER IN YOUR MOUTH.

HOST Frustrated and grieved by the increased burdens in the lives of the chosen people of God, Moses appealed to God for immediate deliverance. And the Lord spoke to Moses and said:

READER Furthermore I have heard the groaning of the sons of Israel, because the Egyptians are holding them in bondage, and I have remembered My covenant. Say, therefore, to the sons of Israel, "I am the LORD, and I will bring you out from under the burdens of the Egyptians, and I will deliver you from their bondage. I will also redeem you with an outstretched arm and with great judgments. Then I will take you for My people, and I will be your God; and you shall know that I am the LORD your God, who brought you out from under the burdens of the Egyptians." (Exodus 6:5–7)

HOST The stage is now set for a mighty act of redemption. We see an obedient servant, a community in agreement, and a God who is faithful. Pharaoh had no regard for God or His people. His grip upon the innocent and helpless people was strong. The people of Israel could not bring about their own freedom. They were helpless under the tyranny of Egypt. The Lord said to Moses:

See, I make you as God to Pharaoh, and your brother Aaron shall be your prophet. You shall speak all that I command you, and your brother Aaron shall speak to Pharaoh that he let the sons of Israel go out of his land. But I will harden Pharaoh's heart that I may multiply My signs and My wonders in the land of Egypt. When Pharaoh does not listen to you, then I will lay My hand on Egypt and bring out My hosts, My people the sons of Israel, from the land of Egypt by great judgments. The Egyptians shall know that I am

the LORD, when I stretch out My hand on Egypt and bring out the sons of Israel from their midst. (Exodus 7:1–5)

 THE PLAGUES

HOST   In every generation it is man's duty to regard himself as though he had personally come out of Egypt, as it is written:

> You shall tell your son on that day, saying, "It is because of what the LORD did for me when I came out of Egypt." [32]

It was not only our fathers whom the Holy One redeemed from slavery; we, too, were redeemed with them, as it is written:

> He brought us out from there in order to bring us in, to give us the land which He had sworn to our fathers. [33]

As we recount His signs and wonders, let us all be reminded of the Lord's awesome power, and His willingness and ability to redeem.

PLAGUE 1
(EXODUS 7:15–25)

The Lord said to Pharaoh through Moses, "Let My people go, that they may serve Me in the wilderness." (v. 16)

Thus says the LORD, "By this you shall know that I am the LORD: behold, I will strike the water that is in the Nile with the staff that is in my hand, and it will be turned to…" (v. 17)

ALL   דָּם   *Dam*
Blood, Blood, Blood

HOST But the magicians of Egypt did the same with their secret arts; and Pharaoh's heart was hardened and he did not listen. (v. 22)

PLAGUE 2
(EXODUS 8:1–15)

Then the Lord said to Moses, "Go to Pharaoh and say to him, 'Thus says the LORD, "Let My people go, that they may serve Me. But if you refuse to let *them* go, behold, I will smite your whole territory with…" ' " (v. 1)

ALL
צְפַרְדֵּעַ *Tzfar'dea*
Frogs, Frogs, Frogs

HOST But the magicians of Egypt did the same with their secret arts. And Pharaoh's heart was hardened. He did not listen.

PLAGUE 3
(EXODUS 8:16–19)

Then the Lord said to Moses, "Say to Aaron, 'Stretch out your staff and strike the dust of the earth, that it may become gnats through all the land of Egypt.'" (v. 16) And he did so, and the dust of the earth became…

ALL
כִּנִּים *Kinim*
Gnats, Gnats, Gnats

HOST The magicians tried with their secret arts to bring forth gnats, but they could not…Then the magicians said to Pharaoh, "This is the finger of God." But Pharaoh's heart was hardened, and he did not listen. (vs. 18–19)

41

 PLAGUE 4
(EXODUS 8:20–32)

The Lord said to Pharaoh through Moses, "Let My people go, that they may serve Me. For if you do not let My people go, behold, I will send swarms of…" (vs. 20–21)

ALL
עָרוֹב *Arov*
Insects, Insects, Insects

HOST Pharaoh's heart was hardened, and he did not listen.

 PLAGUE 5
(EXODUS 9:1–7)

The Lord said to Pharaoh through Moses, "Let My people go, that they may serve Me. For if you refuse to let *them* go and continue to hold them, behold, the hand of the LORD will come *with* a very severe …" (vs. 1–3)

ALL
דֶּבֶר *Dever*
Pestilence, Pestilence, Pestilence

HOST Pharaoh's heart was hardened, and he did not let the people go.

 PLAGUE 6
(EXODUS 9:8–12)

The Lord said, "Take for yourselves handfuls of soot from a kiln, and let Moses throw it toward the sky in the sight of Pharaoh. It will become a fine dust over all the land of Egypt, and will become…" (vs. 1–2)

ALL
שְׁחִין *Sh'chin*
Boils, Boils, Boils

HOST The Lord hardened Pharaoh's heart, and he did not listen to them. (v. 12)

PLAGUE 7
(EXODUS 9:13–35)

The Lord said to Pharaoh through Moses, "Let My people go, that they may serve Me…about this time tomorrow, I will send a very heavy hail, such as has not been *seen* in Egypt from the day it was founded until now."…And the Lord sent… (vs. 13–23)

ALL
בָּרָד *Barad*
Hail, Hail, Hail

HOST The Lord hardened Pharaoh's heart, and he did not let the sons of Israel go.

PLAGUE 8
(EXODUS 10:1–20)

The LORD said to Pharaoh through Moses and Aaron, "How long will you refuse to humble yourself before Me? Let My people go, that they may serve Me…tomorrow I will bring…" (vs. 3–4)

ALL
אַרְבֶּה *Ar'beh*
Locusts, Locusts, Locusts

HOST The Lord hardened Pharaoh's heart, and he did not let the sons of Israel go.

PLAGUE 9
(EXODUS 10:21–29)

The Lord said to Moses, "Stretch out your hand toward the sky, that there may be darkness…even a darkness which may be felt." So Moses stretched out his hand toward the sky, and there was… (vs. 21–22)

ALL
חֹשֶׁךְ *Choshech*
Darkness, Darkness, Darkness

Host Pharaoh's heart became hard and he was not willing to let them go.

Then Pharaoh said to Moses, "Get away from me! Beware, do not see my face again, for in the day you see my face you shall die!" (v. 28) And Moses said, "You are right; I shall never see your face again!" (v. 29)

PLAGUE 10
(EXODUS 11:1–12:31)

The Lord said to Moses, "One more plague I will bring on Pharaoh and on Egypt; after that he will let you go." (11:1) Now it came about on this very night…

All מַכַּת בְּכוֹרוֹת *Makat B'chorot*
Death of the Firstborn

Host Pharaoh called for Moses and Aaron at night and said, "Rise up, get out from among my people, both you and the sons of Israel; and go, worship the LORD, as you have said." (12:31)

This mighty deliverance represents a new life. This is the beginning of the season of springtime, when new growth, life, and freedom await the redeemed.

Reader And you shall observe this event as an ordinance for you and your children forever. When you enter the land which the LORD will give you, as He has promised, you shall observe this rite. And when your children say to you, "What does this rite mean to you?" you shall say, "It is a Passover sacrifice to the LORD who passed over the houses of the sons of Israel in Egypt when He smote the Egyptians, but spared our homes." And the people bowed low and worshiped. (Exodus 12:24–27)

The Second Cup

Deliverance

והצלתי

"I am the LORD, and I
will deliver you from their
bondage."

TAKE THE SECOND CUP AND SAY:

HOST

בָּרוּךְ אַתָּה יהוה
אֱלֹהֵינוּ מֶלֶךְ הָעוֹלָם,
בּוֹרֵא פְּרִי הַגָּפֶן.

Baruch ata Adonai
Eloheinu Melech ha-olam,
borei p'ri hagafen.

ALL Blessed are You, O Lord our God, King of the universe, Who creates the fruit of the vine.

HOST Sanctification is followed by deliverance and redemption, the next two cups of which we will partake.

God has delivered us, and He continues to do so. Before we proceed, let us be quiet before our Maker. Let us consider our lives. Are we sanctified? Are we truly set apart for Him? Or are there other gods in His place? Are there things that we put before Him? Do we have unrepentant, sinful habit patterns in our lives from which we need to be set free?

Take a few moments to be quiet and still before the Lord and meditate on the things from which God desires to set you free. Remember He hears and responds to the cries of His people.

READER Say, therefore, to the sons of Israel, "I am the LORD, and I will bring you out from under the burdens of the Egyptians, and I will deliver you from their bondage. I will also redeem you with an outstretched arm and with great judgments." (Exodus 6:6)

We will not conceal them from their children, but tell to the generation to come the praises of the LORD, and His strength and His wondrous works that He has done. For He established a testimony in Jacob and appointed a law in Israel, which He commanded our fathers, that they should teach them to their children, that the generation to come might know, even the children yet to be born, that they may arise and tell them to their children, that they should put their confidence in God and not

46

forget the works of God, but keep His commandments...
(Psalm 78:3–7)

HOST As sanctified people, we cannot accept sin. The Torah demands our separation from it. It calls for holiness. The Scriptures require a people set free from bondage—a people who respond righteously to God by living holy, sanctified lives. When ready, take the second cup and quietly ask the Father for deliverance in the particular area of your life that He brings to your mind. Read the following prayer to yourself and insert your plea in the indicated area.

INDIVIDUAL PARTICIPANT:
PRAY THIS PRAYER NOW AND SINCERELY ASK GOD
FOR DELIVERANCE FROM A PARTICULAR SIN

🌿 PRAYER FOR DELIVERANCE 🌿

Lord, I have sought my heart and I entreat You to do the same. I come before You tired and weary of carrying the burdens of my sin alone. I need Your deliverance just as the Children of Israel needed Your deliverance. I understand that as I raise this cup in sincerity to You, I am crying out for deliverance from my evil taskmaster. *Abba*, I confess the sin of ....and I ask You, now, to deliver me from this captor. *Abba*, I ask for Your complete and utter deliverance so that I may leave this 'Egypt' and serve You instead. Thank You, Adonai, for providing an escape for me. I delight in your power and authority to accomplish deliverance on my behalf. You are my God, Who has reached out to me with a mighty hand and an outstretched arm. May Your will be done in my life; thank You for Your deliverance.

DRINK THE SECOND CUP

OUT OF EGYPT

HOST   Perhaps the best image of these Passover concepts can be seen in the account of the children of Israel standing against the Red Sea. A vast expanse of impassable water before them, deadly desert on either side, and the fierce Egyptian military in hot pursuit, they faced imminent destruction. At God's command, Moses led them to the edge of the sea, held out his staff, and shouted, "Stand by and see the salvation of the Lord!"[34] At the moment they were faced with utter helplessness, the Lord their God rescued and delivered them.

The children of Israel stood on the banks of the sea, weak and afraid. They could probably see the golden dust of Pharaoh's army off in the distance. Murmuring had already begun. The people began to doubt whether or not God could truly and completely redeem them from their former captors.

There they stood!

ALL   Weak—from their late night and difficult journey.

Frail—from the recent abuse of their taskmasters.

Fearful—that God would not complete their deliverance.

HOST   They needed redemption—a redemption so complete that those in pursuit would never pursue them again.

Listen to the Lord as He speaks words of redemption to His people through His servant Moses:

READER   Do not fear! Stand by and see the salvation of the LORD which He will accomplish for you today; for the Egyptians whom you have seen today, you will never see them again forever. The LORD will fight for you while you keep silent. (Exodus 14:13–14)

HOST   *Redemption had come!* The Lord dealt the final blow that ended the control and intimidation that Pharaoh had on

God's redeemed. In a passionate and joyful celebration, Moses and the people of Israel sang a song to the Lord.[35]

Then Moses and the sons of Israel sang this song to the LORD, and said:

"I will sing to the LORD, for He is highly exalted; The horse and its rider He has hurled into the sea. The LORD is my strength and song, And He has become my salvation; This is my God, and I will praise Him; My father's God, and I will extol Him. The LORD is a warrior; The LORD is His name.

"Pharaoh's chariots and his army He has cast into the sea; And the choicest of his officers are drowned in the Red Sea. The deeps cover them; They went down into the depths like a stone. Your right hand, O LORD, is majestic in power, Your right hand, O LORD, shatters the enemy. And in the greatness of Your excellence You overthrow those who rise up against You; You send forth Your burning anger, and it consumes them as chaff. At the blast of Your nostrils the waters were piled up, The flowing waters stood up like a heap; The deeps were congealed in the heart of the sea.

"The enemy said, 'I will pursue, I will overtake, I will divide the spoil; My desire shall be gratified against them; I will draw out my sword, my hand will destroy them.' You blew with Your wind, the sea covered them; They sank like lead in the mighty waters.

"Who is like You among the gods, O LORD? Who is like You, majestic in holiness, Awesome in praises, working wonders? You stretched out Your right hand, the earth swallowed them.

"In Your lovingkindness You have led the people whom You have redeemed; In Your strength You have guided them to Your holy habitation. The peoples have heard, they tremble; anguish has gripped the inhabitants of

Philistia. Then the chiefs of Edom were dismayed; The leaders of Moab, trembling grips them; All the inhabitants of Canaan have melted away. Terror and dread fall upon them; By the greatness of Your arm they are motionless as stone; Until Your people pass over, O LORD, Until the people pass over whom You have purchased. You will bring them and plant them in the mountain of Your inheritance, The place, O LORD, which You have made for Your dwelling, The sanctuary, O Lord, which Your hands have established. The LORD shall reign forever and ever.

"For the horses of Pharaoh with his chariots and his horsemen went into the sea, and the LORD brought back the waters of the sea on them, but the sons of Israel walked on dry land through the midst of the sea. Miriam the prophetess, Aaron's sister, took the timbrel in her hand, and all the women went out after her with timbrels and with dancing. Miriam answered them", saying…

ALL   "Sing to the LORD, for He is highly exalted; The horse and his rider He has hurled into the sea."

HOST   Just as the Lord delivered Israel from slavery to Egypt, so did He, through Yeshua our Messiah, deliver us from slavery to sin.

> …knowing that you were not redeemed with perishable things like silver or gold…but with precious blood, as of a lamb unblemished and spotless, the blood of the Messiah. (1 Peter 1:18–19)

And just like the children of Israel, who passed through the sea on dry ground,

> We have been buried with Him through baptism (*mikvah*) into death, so that as Messiah was raised from the dead through the glory of the Father, so we too might walk in newness of life. (Romans 6:4)

> But now having been freed from sin and enslaved to God, you derive your benefit, resulting in sanctification, and the outcome, eternal life. (Romans 6:22)

The Third Cup

Redemption

"I am the LORD, and I will
also redeem you with an
outstretched arm and with
great judgments."

TAKE THE THIRD CUP AND SAY:

HOST

בָּרוּךְ אַתָּה יהוה   *Baruch ata Adonai*
אֱלֹהֵינוּ מֶלֶךְ הָעוֹלָם,   *Eloheinu Melech ha-olam,*
בּוֹרֵא פְּרִי הַגָּפֶן.   *borei p'ri hagafen.*

ALL Blessed are You, Lord our God, King of the universe, Who creates the fruit of the vine.

HOST Part of our identity as believers in Yeshua is that we are now redeemed. We are no longer slaves to sin; we are released from its claim. When sin seeks to govern us, we must remember that we walk as redeemed people—because that is who we are in Messiah!

The doctrine of redemption—the releasing of slaves unto freedom—is at the heart and soul of *Pesach*. The slaves were the Israelites; the Egyptians, the cruel masters. The Torah teaches us that Israel's experience as slaves was harsh and brutal. So tyrannized were the children of Israel by their Egyptian taskmasters that they were rendered incapable of redeeming themselves. It took someone other than Israel to bring about their redemption.

In the same way, it is impossible for us to free ourselves from sin. Let us now place our trust in Him to do a work in our lives in the particular areas of bondage (sin) that we are bringing before God.

READER But Moses said to the people, "Do not fear! Stand by and see the salvation of the LORD which He will accomplish for you today; for the Egyptians [world/burden/sin/flesh] whom you have seen today, you will never see them again forever. The LORD will fight for you [redeem you/set you free/sanctify you to be His possession] while *you keep silent*." (Exodus 14:13–14, emphasis and insertions mine)

SONG

SONG #2 : THE LORD KNOWS AND REMEMBERS : PG. 93
OR
SONG #5 : REDEEMER, SAVIOR, FRIEND : PG. 96

INDIVIDUAL PARTICIPANT (PRAYING)
AT ANY TIME DURING THE SONG, TAKE THE THIRD CUP AND PRAY:

> *Abba*, I lift this cup and ask for Your forgiveness for striving in my own strength, for not depending upon You, and for violating Your ways. I ask that You sanctify me, deliverer me, redeem me.

DRINK THE THIRD CUP

DAYEINU
(IT WOULD HAVE BEEN ENOUGH)

HOST God has bestowed many favors upon us. Let us recall these works in the traditional reading of the *Dayeinu*[36] and worship our God, who delivers His people.

Had He brought us out of Egypt and not executed judgments against the Egyptians, it would have been enough.

ALL דַּיֵּינוּ *Dayeinu*

HOST Had He executed judgments against the Egyptians and not their gods, it would have been enough.

ALL דַּיֵּינוּ *Dayeinu*

HOST Had He executed judgments against their gods and not put to death their firstborn, it would have been enough.

ALL דַּיֵּינוּ *Dayeinu*

HOST Had He put to death their firstborn and not given us their riches, it would have been enough.

ALL דַּיֵּינוּ *Dayeinu*

HOST Had He given us their riches and not split the sea for us, it would have been enough.

ALL דַּיֵּינוּ *Dayeinu*

HOST Had He split the sea for us and not led us through it on dry land, it would have been enough.

ALL דַּיֵּינוּ *Dayeinu*

HOST Had He led us through it on dry land and not sunk our foes in it, it would have been enough.

ALL דַּיֵּינוּ *Dayeinu*

HOST Had He sunk our foes in it and not satisfied our needs in the desert for forty years, it would have been enough.

ALL דַּיֵּינוּ *Dayeinu*

HOST Had He satisfied our needs in the desert for forty years and not fed us the manna, it would have been enough.

ALL דַּיֵּינוּ *Dayeinu*

HOST Had He fed us the manna and not given us the Sabbath, it would have been enough.

ALL דַּיֵּינוּ *Dayeinu*

HOST Had He given us the Sabbath and not brought us to Mount Sinai, it would have been enough.

ALL דַּיֵּינוּ *Dayeinu*

HOST Had He brought us to Mount Sinai and not given us the Torah, it would have been enough.

ALL דַּיֵּינוּ *Dayeinu*

HOST Had He given us the Torah and not brought us into Israel, it would have been enough.

ALL דַּיֵּינוּ *Dayeinu*

HOST How much more so, then, should we be grateful to God for the numerous favors that He bestowed upon us: He brought us out of Egypt and punished the Egyptians; He smote their gods and slew their firstborn; He gave us their wealth and split the sea for us; He led us through it on dry land and sank our foes in it; He sustained us in the desert for forty years and fed us with the manna; He gave us the *Shabbat* and brought us to Mount Sinai; He gave us the Torah and brought us to Israel; He gave us His Son to redeem us from death; He raised Him again and atoned for all our sins. In Messiah, He gives abundance; in Yeshua, eternal life.

✾ DAYEINU ✾

אִלּוּ הוֹצִיאָנוּ מִמִּצְרַיִם	*Ilu hotzianu mi'mitzrayim*
וְלֹא עָשָׂה בָהֶם שְׁפָטִים	*v'lo asa vahem sh'phatim*
דַּיֵּינוּ.	*dayeinu.*
אִלּוּ עָשָׂה בָהֶם שְׁפָטִים	*Ilu asa vahem sh'phatim*
וְלֹא עָשָׂה בֵאלֹהֵיהֶם	*v'lo asa veloheihem*
דַּיֵּינוּ.	*dayeinu.*
אִלּוּ עָשָׂה בֵאלֹהֵיהֶם	*Ilu asa veloheihem*
וְלֹא הָרַג אֶת בְּכוֹרֵיהֶם	*v'lo harag et b'choreihem*
דַּיֵּינוּ.	*dayeinu.*
אִלּוּ הָרַג אֶת בְּכוֹרֵיהֶם	*Ilu harag et b'choreihem*
וְלֹא נָתַן לָנוּ אֶת מָמוֹנָם	*v'lo natan lanu et ma'monam*
דַּיֵּינוּ.	*dayeinu.*
אִלּוּ נָתַן לָנוּ אֶת מָמוֹנָם	*Ilu natan lanu et ma'monam*
וְלֹא קָרַע לָנוּ אֶת הַיָּם	*v'lo kara lanu et ha'yam*
דַּיֵּינוּ.	*dayeinu.*

אִלּוּ קָרַע לָנוּ אֶת הַיָּם	Ilu kara lanu et ha'yam
וְלֹא הֶעֱבִירָנוּ בְתוֹכוֹ בֶּחָרָבָה	v'lo hei'viranu v'tocho beicharava
דַּיֵּנוּ.	dayeinu.
אִלּוּ הֶעֱבִירָנוּ בְתוֹכוֹ בֶּחָרָבָה	Ilu he'eviranu v'tocho beicharava
וְלֹא שִׁקַּע צָרֵינוּ בְתוֹכוֹ	v'lo shika tzareinu v'tocho
דַּיֵּנוּ.	dayeinu.
אִלּוּ שִׁקַּע צָרֵינוּ בְתוֹכוֹ	Ilu shika tzareinu v'tocho
וְלֹא סִפֵּק צָרְכֵּינוּ בַּמִּדְבָּר	v'lo sipek tzar'cheinu bamidbar
אַרְבָּעִים שָׁנָה	ar'ba'im shana
דַּיֵּנוּ,	dayeinu.
אִלּוּ סִפֵּק צָרְכֵּינוּ בַּמִּדְבָּר	Ilu sipek tzar'cheinu bamidbar
אַרְבָּעִים שָׁנָה	ar'ba'im shana
וְלֹא הֶאֱכִילָנוּ אֶת הַמָּן	v'lo hei'chilanu et haman
דַּיֵּנוּ.	dayeinu.
אִלּוּ הֶאֱכִילָנוּ אֶת הַמָּן	Ilu hei'chilanu et haman
וְלֹא נָתַן לָנוּ אֶת הַשַּׁבָּת	v'lo natan lanu et ha'shabbat
דַּיֵּנוּ.	dayeinu.
אִלּוּ נָתַן לָנוּ אֶת הַשַּׁבָּת	Ilu natan lanu et ha'shabbat
וְלֹא קֵרְבָנוּ לִפְנֵי הַר סִינַי,	v'lo ker'vanu liph'nei har sinai
דַּיֵּנוּ.	dayeinu.
אִלּוּ קֵרְבָנוּ לִפְנֵי הַר סִינַי	Ilu ker'vanu liph'nei har sinai
וְלֹא נָתַן לָנוּ אֶת הַתּוֹרָה	v'lo natan lanu et torah
דַּיֵּנוּ.	dayeinu.
אִלּוּ נָתַן לָנוּ אֶת הַתּוֹרָה	Ilu natan lanu et torah
וְלֹא הִכְנִיסָנוּ לְאֶרֶץ יִשְׂרָאֵל	v'lo hich'nisanu l'eretz yisrael,
דַּיֵּנוּ.	dayeinu.
אִלּוּ הִכְנִיסָנוּ לְאֶרֶץ יִשְׂרָאֵל	Ilu hich'nisanu l'eretz yisrael,
וְלֹא בָנָה לָנוּ אֶת בֵּית הַבְּחִירָה	v'lo vana lanu et beit ha'b'chira
דַּיֵּנוּ.	dayeinu.

✣ With True Freedom Comes Life ✣

HOST   God does not just redeem—He gives life. God heard the cry of His people; He redeemed them and sovereignly moved on their behalf. Once they were free to serve Him, Adonai betrothed His people Israel and gave them words of life.

> "You yourselves have seen what I did to the Egyptians, and how I bore you on eagles' wings, and brought you to Myself. Now then, if you will indeed obey My voice and keep My covenant, then you shall be My own possession among all the peoples, for all the earth is Mine; and you shall be to Me a kingdom of priests and a holy nation." These are the words that you shall speak to the sons of Israel. (Exodus 19:4–6)

ALL   Then God said all these words. "I am the LORD your God, who brought you out of the land of Egypt, out of the house of slavery." (Exodus 20:2)

READER   …indeed, we had the sentence of death within ourselves so that we would not trust in ourselves, but in God who raises the dead; who delivered us from so great a peril of death, and will deliver us, He on whom we have set our hope. And He will yet deliver us… (2 Corinthians 1:9–10)

ALL   "You are to have no other gods before me." (Exodus 20:3)

READER   "You shall not make for yourself an idol, or any likeness of what is in heaven above or on the earth beneath or in the water under the earth. You shall not worship them or serve them; for I, the LORD your God, am a jealous God, visiting the iniquity of the fathers on the children, on the third and the fourth generations of those who hate Me, but showing lovingkindness to thousands, to those who love Me and keep My commandments." (Exodus 20:4–6)

ALL   "You shall not take the name of the LORD your God in vain…" (Exodus 20:7)

READER	"For the LORD will not leave him unpunished who takes His name in vain." (Exodus 20:7) "Let the name of God be blessed forever and ever, for wisdom and power belong to Him." (Daniel 2:20)
ALL	"Remember the Sabbath day, to keep it holy." (Exodus 20:8)
READER	"Six days you shall labor and do all your work, but the seventh day is a Sabbath of the LORD your God; in it you shall not do any work, you or your son or your daughter or your male servant or your female servant or your ox or your donkey or any of your cattle or your sojourner who stays with you, so that your male servant and your female servant may rest as well as you. You shall remember that you were a slave in the land of Egypt, and the LORD your God brought you out of there by a mighty hand and by an outstretched arm; therefore the LORD your God commanded you to observe the Sabbath day." (Deuteronomy 5:13–15)
ALL	"Honor your father and mother, that your days may be prolonged in the land which the LORD your God gives you." (Exodus 20:12)
READER	Hear, my son, your father's instruction, and do not forsake your mother's teaching; indeed, they are a graceful wreath to your head, and ornaments about your neck. (Proverbs 1:8–9)
ALL	"You shall not murder." (Exodus 20:13)
READER	Whoever sheds man's blood, by man his blood shall be shed, for in the image of God He made man. (Genesis 9:6)
ALL	"You shall not commit adultery." (Exodus 20:14)
READER	For this is the will of God, your sanctification; that is, that you abstain from sexual immorality; that each of you know how to possess his own vessel in sanctification and honor,

not in lustful passion, like the Gentiles who do not know God… (1 Thessalonians 4:3–5)

ALL   "You shall not steal." (Exodus 20:15)

READER   He who steals must steal no longer; but rather he must labor, performing with his own hands what is good, so that he will have something to share with one who has need. (Ephesians 4:28)

ALL   "You shall not bear false witness against your neighbor." (Exodus 20:16)

READER   There are six things which the LORD hates, Yes, seven which are an abomination to Him: Haughty eyes, a lying tongue, And hands that shed innocent blood, A heart that devises wicked plans, Feet that run rapidly to evil, A false witness who utters lies, And one who spreads strife among brothers. (Proverbs 6:16–19)

ALL   "You shall not covet your neighbor's house; you shall not covet your neighbor's wife… or anything that belongs to your neighbor." (Exodus 20:17)

READER   But each one is tempted when he is carried away and enticed by his own lust. Then when lust has conceived, it gives birth to sin; and when sin is accomplished, it brings forth death. (James 1:14–15)

HOST   God separated Israel from the burden of the Egyptians. His purpose in doing so was that Israel might worship Him unfettered. Each time the famous line is spoken, "Let My people go," it is followed with "so that they might serve Me."

READER   For the grace of God has appeared, bringing salvation to all men, instructing us to deny ungodliness and worldly desires and to live sensibly, righteously and godly in the present age, looking for the blessed hope and the appearing of the glory of our great God and Savior, Messiah Yeshua, who gave Himself for us to redeem us from

every lawless deed, and to purify for Himself a people for His own possession, zealous for good deeds. These things speak and exhort and reprove with all authority. Let no one disregard you. (Titus 2:11–15)

The Fourth Cup

Hope

וְלָקַחְתִּי

"I am the LORD, and I will take you for
My people, and I will be your God; and
you shall know that I am the LORD your
God, who brought you out from under the
burdens of the Egyptians."

HOST It is with great hope that we take this last cup. Let us proclaim together with one voice:

ALL

בָּרוּךְ אַתָּה יהוה   *Baruch ata Adonai*
אֱלֹהֵינוּ מֶלֶךְ הָעוֹלָם,   *Eloheinu Melech ha-olam,*
בּוֹרֵא פְּרִי הַגָּפֶן.   *borei p'ri hagafen.*

Blessed are You, Lord our God, King of the universe, Who creates the fruit of the vine.

Adonai, You have indeed called us forth. You have chosen us. You have redeemed us. You have lavished Your grace upon us and have given us Your Torah, and You have called us to shine Your light. May we reflect to the nations around us that we are Your redeemed people—a holy and set-apart people.

DRINK THE FOURTH CUP

READER The LORD has today declared you to be His people, a treasured possession, as He promised you, and that you should keep all His commandments; and that He will set you high above all nations which He has made, for praise, fame, and honor; and that you shall be a consecrated people to the LORD your God, as He has spoken. (Deuteronomy 26:18–19)

HOST In this Scripture we see that an inherent part of being the Lord's chosen one is to be a "holy people…to your God." To be His means to be like Him, to reflect His image, and to "keep all His commandments." (Deuteronomy 7:6; 26:18)

It is our solemn prayer that the people of God have an increased awareness of belonging to Adonai, which influences not only our lifestyles, but also our love and dedication to Him.

The cup of hope also looks to the future, to the return of Messiah as declared by the prophet Elijah. So with this cup we look to the time in which our final redemption will come and we will be truly sanctified, delivered, and redeemed.

 A NEW BATCH

RAISING THE MATZAH, THE HOST DECLARES:

HOST Just as our ancestors left their leaven in Egypt, so do we leave our old ways behind. In the newness of our redemption, let us eat the unleavened bread now and for the next seven days, and may it remind us of who we really are, set free to be in the Messiah Yeshua.

בָּרוּךְ אַתָּה יהוה *Baruch ata Adonai*
אֱלֹהֵינוּ מֶלֶךְ הָעוֹלָם, *Eloheinu Melech ha-olam,*
הַמּוֹצִיא לֶחֶם *hamotzi lechem*
מִן הָאָרֶץ. *min ha-aretz.*

ALL Blessed are You, Lord our God, King of the universe, Who brings forth bread from the earth.

בָּרוּךְ אַתָּה יהוה *Baruch ata Adonai*
אֱלֹהֵינוּ מֶלֶךְ הָעוֹלָם, *Eloheinu Melech ha-olam,*
אֲשֶׁר קִדְּשָׁנוּ בְּמִצְוֹתָיו *asher kid'shanu b'mitz'votav*
וְצִוָּנוּ עַל אֲכִילַת מַצָּה. *v'tzivanu al achilat matza.*

ALL Blessed are You, Lord our God, Who has sanctified us with Your commandments, and commanded us to eat unleavened bread.

 SONG

SONG #3 : THE MIKVAH SONG : PG. 94
OR
SONG #6 : I WILL NEVER BE THE SAME AGAIN : PG. 97

Abba, You made me new. You have delivered me, You redeemed me, You have sanctified me and set me apart for Yourself. Abba, You have set me free, and from this moment on, I will never be the same again.

🌿 FELLOWSHIP MEAL 🌿

Host Remaining in a sober, reflective spirit, let us now partake of a fellowship meal with one another. Let our words be words of remembrance and not of our common lives. Let us remain in the spirit of the evening.

CONTINUE HERE AFTER THE FELLOWSHIP MEAL

Host Blessed are You, Lord our God, King of the universe, who nourishes the whole world with grace, kindness, and mercy. You give food to all creatures, for Your kindness endures forever. Through this great goodness we have never been in want; may we never be in want of sustenance for Your great name's sake. You are the God who sustains all, does good to all, and provides food for all the creatures which You have created. Blessed are You, O Lord, who sustains all.

We thank You, Lord our God, for having given a beautiful, good, and spacious land to our fathers as a heritage; for having taken us out, Lord our God, from the land of Egypt and redeeming us from the house of slavery. for Your covenant, which You have sealed in our flesh; for your Torah, which You have taught us; for Your statues, which You have made known to us; for the life, grace, and kindness You have bestowed on us; and for the food with which You sustain us at all times.

For everything, Lord our God, we thank You and bless You. May Your name be constantly blessed by all forever, as it is written: "When you have eaten and are satisfied, you shall bless the LORD your God for the good land which He has given you." (Deuteronomy 8:10) Blessed art You, O Lord, for the land and the food.

ALL Amen.

 THE GREAT HALLEL

HOST Praised be Your name forever, our King who rules and is great and holy in heaven and on earth. For to You, Lord our God, it is fitting to render song and praise, Hallel and psalms, power and dominion, victory, glory and might, praise and beauty, holiness and sovereignty, blessings and thanks, from now and forever. All Your works praise You, Lord our God. Your pious followers who perform Your will, and all Your people, the house of Israel, praise, thank, bless, glorify, extol, exalt, revere, sanctify, and coronate Your name, our King. To You it is fitting to give thanks, and unto Your name it is proper to sing praises, for You are God eternal.

HOST Give thanks to the LORD, for He is good;

ALL כִּי לְעוֹלָם חַסְדּוֹ *Ki l'olam chasdo*
for His lovingkindness is everlasting.

HOST Give thanks to the God of gods,

ALL כִּי לְעוֹלָם חַסְדּוֹ *Ki l'olam chasdo*
for His lovingkindness is everlasting.

HOST Give thanks to the Lord of lords,

ALL כִּי לְעוֹלָם חַסְדּוֹ *Ki l'olam chasdo*
for His lovingkindness is everlasting.

HOST To Him who alone does great wonders,

ALL כִּי לְעוֹלָם חַסְדּוֹ *Ki l'olam chasdo*
for His lovingkindness is everlasting.

HOST To Him who made the heavens with skill,

ALL כִּי לְעוֹלָם חַסְדּוֹ *Ki l'olam chasdo*
for His lovingkindness is everlasting.

HOST To Him who spread out the earth above the waters,

ALL כִּי לְעוֹלָם חַסְדּוֹ *Ki l'olam chasdo*
for His lovingkindness is everlasting.

HOST To Him who made the great lights,

ALL כִּי לְעוֹלָם חַסְדּוֹ *Ki l'olam chasdo*
for His lovingkindness is everlasting.

HOST The sun to rule by day,

ALL כִּי לְעוֹלָם חַסְדּוֹ *Ki l'olam chasdo*
for His lovingkindness is everlasting.

HOST The moon and stars to rule by night,

ALL כִּי לְעוֹלָם חַסְדּוֹ *Ki l'olam chasdo*
for His lovingkindness is everlasting.

HOST To Him who smote the Egyptians in their firstborn,

ALL כִּי לְעוֹלָם חַסְדּוֹ *Ki l'olam chasdo*
for His lovingkindness is everlasting.

HOST And brought Israel out from their midst,

ALL כִּי לְעוֹלָם חַסְדּוֹ *Ki l'olam chasdo*
for His lovingkindness is everlasting.

HOST With a strong hand and an outstretched arm,

ALL כִּי לְעוֹלָם חַסְדּוֹ *Ki l'olam chasdo*
for His lovingkindness is everlasting.

HOST   To Him who divided the Red Sea asunder,

ALL   כִּי לְעוֹלָם חַסְדּוֹ   *Ki l'olam chasdo*
        for His lovingkindness is everlasting.

HOST   And made Israel pass through the midst of it,

ALL   כִּי לְעוֹלָם חַסְדּוֹ   *Ki l'olam chasdo*
        for His lovingkindness is everlasting.

HOST   But He overthrew Pharaoh and his army in the Red Sea,

ALL   כִּי לְעוֹלָם חַסְדּוֹ   *Ki l'olam chasdo*
        for His lovingkindness is everlasting.

HOST   To Him who led His people through the wilderness,

ALL   כִּי לְעוֹלָם חַסְדּוֹ   *Ki l'olam chasdo*
        for His lovingkindness is everlasting.

HOST   To Him who smote great kings,

ALL   כִּי לְעוֹלָם חַסְדּוֹ   *Ki l'olam chasdo*
        for His lovingkindness is everlasting.

HOST   And slew mighty kings,

ALL   כִּי לְעוֹלָם חַסְדּוֹ   *Ki l'olam chasdo*
        for His lovingkindness is everlasting.

HOST   And gave their land as a heritage,

ALL   כִּי לְעוֹלָם חַסְדּוֹ   *Ki l'olam chasdo*
        for His lovingkindness is everlasting.

HOST   Even a heritage to Israel His servant,

ALL   כִּי לְעוֹלָם חַסְדּוֹ   *Ki l'olam chasdo*
        for His lovingkindness is everlasting.

HOST   Who remembered us in our low estate,

ALL   כִּי לְעוֹלָם חַסְדּוֹ   *Ki l'olam chasdo*
        for His lovingkindness is everlasting.

67

HOST And has rescued us from our adversaries,

ALL כִּי לְעוֹלָם חַסְדּוֹ *Ki l'olam chasdo*
for His lovingkindness is everlasting.

HOST Who gives food to all flesh,

ALL כִּי לְעוֹלָם חַסְדּוֹ *Ki l'olam chasdo*
for His lovingkindness is everlasting.

HOST Give thanks to the God of heaven,

ALL כִּי לְעוֹלָם חַסְדּוֹ *Ki l'olam chasdo*
for His lovingkindness is everlasting.

COMMEMORATION COMPLETED

WE CLOSE THIS *SEDER* WITH THE PLEA:

HOST Master, we ask that You return. We ask that You reestablish Your throne in Jerusalem, Your holy city. We appeal to You now to bring Your righteous rules, statutes, and judgments by restoring Your kingdom. So we shout out for our redemption, and may we all be…

NEXT YEAR IN YERUSHALAIM

ALL לְשָׁנָה הַבָּאָה בִּירוּשָׁלָיִם
L'shana Haba'a Birushalaim

HOST Lord, though You tarry, allow us to enter into this new year, this time of new life, new growth, and a new beginning of Your redemptive cycle. May this year be for us one of growth, prosperity, and health.

Amen.

🌿 Personal Reflections 🌿

Suggestions for Families and Children

Bedikat Chametz
"The Check for Leaven"

In preparation for Passover and the Feast of Unleavened Bread, God commands His people to remove the *chametz* (leaven) from their dwelling places and to eat unleavened bread for seven days.

> Seven days there shall be no leaven found in your houses; for whoever eats what is leavened, that person shall be cut off from the congregation of Israel, whether he is an alien or a native of the land. You shall not eat anything leavened; in all your dwellings you shall eat unleavened bread. (Exodus 12:19–20)

Preparation for this appointed time often begins a month early with a thorough spring cleaning. Houses are cleaned from basement to attic in order to search each nook and cranny for any traces of *chametz* (leaven). A traditional Jewish custom in this yearly ritual preparation for Passover is *Bedikat Chametz*, "a check for leaven." On the eve before Passover begins, and after the house has been meticulously cleaned, the final search for leaven is conducted.

Customarily, one slice of bread is cut into ten small pieces and hidden in the home where the *chametz* may have been stored in the previous year. Eager children join with their parents to search the home by candlelight, looking for any *chametz* that remains in the home. The pieces of *chametz* are located and brushed onto a wooden spoon with a feather. When all ten pieces are found, the candle, feather, wooden spoon, and *chametz* are tied together and placed outside of the home in order to fulfill the commandment of removing all leaven from the dwelling place. Traditionally this bundle is burned prior to the *seder*.

We have modified this custom in order to provide you with an engaging activity and spiritual applications that lead your family to prepare for the Passover season by contemplating the atonement provided in Messiah Yeshua.

For the first part of this activity, you will need a few items:

- Bible
- Candle or flashlight
- Feather
- Wooden spoon
- Linen cloth or large paper napkin
- String
- One slice of bread, cut into ten small cubes

Before you begin the activity as a family, you will need to hide the ten small cubes of bread for the children to find. Dim the lights in your home, gather your family together, and open the activity with prayer. When you are prepared to begin the activity read Exodus 12:19–20 and the description of *Bedikat Chametz* for your family members. You may desire to recite the traditional Hebrew prayer before the search commences:

בָּרוּךְ אַתָּה יהוה   *Baruch ata Adonai*
אֱלֹהֵינוּ מֶלֶךְ הָעוֹלָם,   *Eloheinu Melech ha-olam,*
אֲשֶׁר קִדְּשָׁנוּ בְּמִצְוֹתָיו   *asher kid'shanu b'mitz,votav*
וְצִוָּנוּ עַל בִּיעוּר חָמֵץ.   *v'tzivanu al biur chametz.*

Blessed are You, Lord our God, King of the Universe, Who has sanctified us with His commandments and commanded us concerning the removal of *chametz*.

Have an older child hold the candle or flashlight to search for the *chametz* (bread cubes) and another use the feather to scoop the leaven into the wooden spoon. Parents may need to give hints to help locate. Place each bread cube in the paper napkin until the children have found all ten pieces. Blow out the candle and set aside along with the feather, wooden spoon, and napkin filled with bread crumbs for later use in the completion of this activity. Gather together as a family for study and discussion using the questions provided.

QUESTIONS

- Read 1 Corinthians 5:6–8. What feast is Paul speaking of in this passage?
- What happens when a small amount of leaven is introduced to the dough?
- What is to be done with the old leaven?
- What does the old leaven represent?
- What does the unleavened bread represent?
- Read 1 John 3:4. How does the Bible define sin?
- Does a small amount of sin bring harm in one's life?
- How does the Bible define righteousness?
- How are we to be cleansed from sin and made new?
- Read Psalm 26:2 and 2 Corinthians 13:5. How can we examine our lives (minds and hearts) to see if we have sinful habits, thoughts, or behaviors (leaven) in our own lives that need to be removed?

SPIRITUAL APPLICATION

Note: The following is intended to be a time of reflection and repentance; however, as parents you may want to spend additional time in discussion or prayer with your children about issues related to sin before proceeding with this activity.

For the second half of this activity, you will need:

- Bible
- Picture of lamb for each person
- Red Pen
- Cotton Balls
- Glue

- Read and discuss Isaiah 1:18: "Though your sins are as scarlet, they will be as white as snow; though they are red like crimson, they will be like wool."

- Read John 1:29. What did John state about Messiah Yeshua?

- Discuss how Messiah's atonement provides redemption from sin. Lead your family to privately consider any sinful habits, thoughts, or behaviors, which are symbolized by leaven, that may exist in their lives as well as your own.

- Read 1 John 1:1–10. Ask each family member to individually record his/her personal sins or areas of repetitive sinful behavior on the lamb picture with a red pen in remembrance that sin is a stain as scarlet upon our lives.

- Read Isaiah 53. Discuss how Messiah bore our transgressions. Spend a few moments in private or corporate prayer and repentance as needed by your family for the sins that were recorded on the lamb.

- Read Psalm 103. Discuss how the Lord completely removes sin. Glue cotton balls on the body of the lamb, covering the sins listed in red ink.

- Take the lamb pictures with the materials from the *Bedikat Chametz* (candle, feather, wooden spoon, and bread cubes), and wrap them together in a linen cloth or large napkin. Tie it all together with string and set by the entrance to your home to discard before the Passover and the Feast of Unleavened Bread begins. End this activity with a family time of prayer and thanksgiving.

Passover Bibliodrama

As you prepare for the Passover *seder* and the Feast of Unleavened Bread, take time to consider how you can impart these spiritual truths to your children so that they will, in turn, relate them to their children. Your efforts to teach a heritage of faith in this generation will affect the generations to come for righteousness' sake.

One biblical injunction concerning Passover is to observe the event in all generations as recorded in the Torah:

> And you shall observe this event as an ordinance for you and your children forever. When you enter the land which the LORD will give you, as He has promised, you shall observe this rite. And when your children say to you, "What does this rite mean to you?" you shall say, "It is a Passover sacrifice to the LORD who passed over the houses of the sons of Israel in Egypt when He smote the Egyptians, but spared our homes." (Exodus 12:25–27)

Furthermore, Jewish tradition teaches that,

> In every generation, each individual should feel as though he or she has gone out of Egypt. (Traditional Passover *Haggadah*)

The *Passover Encounter seder* is geared to be experienced as a community. Therefore, you may want to spiritually prepare your children for this event beforehand. You may wish to engage the following dramatization in your home the evening prior to the *seder*. The activity provided will help you reenact the first Passover, when Israelite families were protected in their homes by the blood of the Passover lamb, which was applied to their doorposts.

This dramatization, or bibliodrama, provides your family with an opportunity to study the Passover account in Exodus while learning spiritual truths. You can create an atmosphere in your home that allows your family to experience what it must have been like that first Passover eve. Through engaging in a short study and discussion, your family will be led to contemplate the atoning work and redemption given through Messiah Yeshua—the Passover Lamb.

To prepare for the reenactment of the original Passover, you will need to gather a few materials:

- Passover Encounter CD
- CD player
- Votives with candles
- Long strips of brown construction paper
- Scotch tape
- Heavy paper or cardboard for doorposts
- Washable red paint
- Small basin or bowl
- Paintbrush decorated with a hyssop stalk made of construction paper
- Simple biblical garments (tunics, sandals, packs for journey, walking sticks)

Prepare for the bibliodrama by choosing an area within your home that you can set up as a dining area and select a doorway to serve as the entrance for the Hebrew dwelling. Affix the heavy paper or cardboard to the lintel and doorposts that will be used during the bibliodrama. You may want to use a low table and arrange seating with cushions on the floor for the dinner. Plan to prepare a simple meal along with the biblical elements mentioned in Exodus 12, including unleavened bread, bitter herbs, and a shank bone of a lamb to symbolize the *pesach* sacrifice.

The most appropriate time for the bibliodrama to be held is the twilight of the evening, just like the *seder* itself. Dim the lights in the room and arrange votive candles to symbolize the lights of the Hebrew dwelling places in Egypt (Exodus 10:23). Place the CD player in the room in an inconspicuous area and queue the *Passover Encounter* CD to the Passover narrative by D. Thomas Lancaster to be used at an appropriate time during the bibliodrama. Dress in simple biblical garments and finish final preparations for the dinner. The simple meal should be served family-style so that all members of the family can sit at the low table and listen to the narration of Passover.

Begin the evening by stepping outside of your home to view the sky. The people of Israel have commemorated Passover for thousands of years under the full moon of Nisan 14. On a clear evening, you should be able to view a nearly full moon (if you have your bibliodrama near the actual date of Passover). Gather your family together at the doorway of the dwelling area where the meal will be served. Give each family member a shackle made from a long strip of brown construction paper and place it around his or her ankle and secure with tape to symbolize slavery in Egypt. Read Exodus 12:1–14; 21–23 aloud. Apply the blood of the lamb (washable red paint) to the lintel and doorposts of the house or room by using the hyssop stalk (decorated paintbrush). Enter the room and be seated at the low table for dinner. While eating dinner, listen to the Passover narrative on CD and reflect upon the account of the Passover and the deliverance of the Israelites from the bondage and oppression of Egypt.

After listening to the Passover narrative, prepare your family to exit the room, symbolizing when the Israelites left Egypt in haste. As you leave the room, have each person remove and discard the shackle of slavery around his or her ankle. Gather together in a nearby room to participate in a short study and discussion.

Questions for Discussion

Encourage the children to share their thoughts and questions of the Passover. Discuss with the children why the Passover night was different from all other nights. What is the importance of Passover and teaching each generation about the great Exodus from Egypt?

Chapters 12 and 13 of Exodus give many important instructions regarding Passover and the Feast of Unleavened Bread. See how many answers your children can recall.

- What kind of lambs were to be used for the Passover sacrifice?
- How did God command the Passover lamb to be prepared?
- Where was the blood of the lamb to be placed?

- What would happen if the Israelites neglected to follow God's instructions?

- What occurred at midnight in Egypt? How did Pharaoh respond?

- How were the Hebrews protected from the tragedies in Egypt?

- Why did the Israelites make their bread without leaven?

- How many days did God command His people to eat unleavened bread?

- For how long should the Passover continued to be observed?

- Why should we as followers of Messiah Yeshua obey all of God's instructions?

SPIRITUAL APPLICATION

- Read aloud Matthew 26:1–30 and discuss the last *seder* meal Messiah Yeshua shared with His disciples before He became the Passover Lamb who "takes away the sin of the world." (John 1:29)

- What did Yeshua say the unleavened bread represented?

- What did Yeshua say the cup represented?

- Contemplate the transformation and redemption Messiah has brought about in your own life. Oftentimes, Egypt is spiritually symbolized as the bondage of sin. Discuss how through the atoning work of Messiah Yeshua we attain our freedom from the bondage to sin and are delivered from the wages of sin, which is death. Remember the shackle, which you removed from your ankle, which symbolized slavery in Egypt, and give thanks to God for delivering you from darkness. Give each family member an opportunity to thank God for the redemption and freedom that He has provided.

- Remind your children that they will be participating the next evening in a Passover *seder* to commemorate the story of God's salvation, the Exodus from Egypt, and the redemption provided through Messiah Yeshua. Explain to your children that according to the biblical mandate of Exodus 12:25–27 and the Sages of Israel, they will be the most honored guests at the Passover *seder* as they will relate the story of God's salvation to the following generations.
- Close the evening by saying a special prayer and blessing over your children.

Additional Ideas for the Bibliodrama

This bibliodrama can be modified to be as simple or elaborate as your family desires. Let your creativity flow. Create a sense of anticipation, excitement, and wonder within your home as you recount the first Passover night and the Exodus from Egypt.

Other ideas:

- Designate a doorway to be an exit from the Bibliodrama and decorate it to commemorate the crossing of the Red Sea. You might use blue streamers or fabric. The children will enjoy decorating pictures of fish and other sea life to place around the door. You could also have ocean sounds playing on a small CD player.
- Create a mural of an Egyptian scene (pyramids, etc.) outside of the Passover door to symbolize the life of slavery in Egypt.
- The day of the bibliodrama, you could set up an activity outside of the house and have the children make bricks from mud and straw.

CRAFT: BIBLICAL TUNIC

It is easy for children to create simple biblical tunics from colored or striped cloth. You may even use sheets or burlap. Use the following measurements, and cut a simple rectangle from your materials.

- ❧ Adults—40"x 64"
- ❧ S Youth—24"x 48"
- ❧ M Youth—28"x 60"
- ❧ L Youth—30"x 64"
- ❧ XL Youth—36"x 64"

Fold the rectangle in half. Cut a neck opening at the fold. Slip tunic over your head and tie at the waist with jute cord, rope, or surplus material. This garment can be worn without sewing to keep the activity simple. However, you may desire to sew side seams on this garment to allow room for armholes.

ACTIVITY: UNLEAVENED BREAD

For seven days during Passover and the Feast of Unleavened Bread, we eat bread made without leavening. Leavening is a substance that produces the fermentation process and includes yeast, baking powder, and baking soda. These normally cause bread to rise to a fluffy texture. Without these agents, bread remains flat after baking. Eating this bread reminds us of the Israelites who ate the Passover in haste before they departed from Egypt, and enables us to fulfill God's commandment to eat unleavened bread for the seven days of the appointed time.

These simple recipes can be prepared by children with adult assistance.

SEPHARDIC (SPANISH/PORTUGUESE) UNLEAVENED BREAD
Ingredients:

2 cups of Masa Harina (corn flour)

1¼ to 1½ cups of warm water

½ tsp sea salt

Mix the Masa Harina and water and knead to form soft dough. You may need to add a bit of water or additional masa to reach the right consistency. Divide and form mixture into golf-ball-size sections. Roll each section into a flat tortilla, and transfer to a hot, dry skillet. Cook for 30 seconds on one side, turn tortilla, and cook for 60 seconds. Turn again to finish cooking first side 30 seconds. You may keep the tortillas warm in a 250-degree oven.

ASHKENAZIC (EASTERN EUROPEAN) UNLEAVENED BREAD

Ingredients:
    3 cups of the flour of your choice
    3 tbsp olive oil
    2 tbsp honey
    2 eggs
    ½ cup warm water
    1 tsp sea salt

Preheat your oven to 450 degrees. Combine the dry ingredients in a medium bowl. Add eggs, oil, honey, and water to the flour mixture and knead until smooth. Divide and form mixture into golf-ball-size sections with hands greased with olive oil. On a floured surface, roll each ball into flat, round circles. If you would like the dough to bake crisper, prick holes in the surface; otherwise, it will bake as thicker flatbread. Place on a pan or stone in oven and bake for 20 minutes.

Preparation for Pesach

ENVIRONMENT AND TIMING

Pesach is a special time. Special dishes, fresh flowers, and nice clothing all set the environment for a wonderful occasion. This is an appointment with God, so give yourself ample time to prepare. You do not want to rush into this time. Traditionally, thorough housecleaning and *seder* preparations begin several weeks ahead of time.

Moms and daughters prepare the meal, young boys assist in the areas of need, and fathers review and prepare the "telling." We can easily get caught up in preparations and find ourselves rushing into the appointment rather than fostering a peaceful and spiritually conducive environment. In terms of God's appointed feasts, timing is everything.

THE MIKVAH

In the days of the Temple, worshipers would prepare to participate in the *seder* meal by going through a ritual immersion in a *mikvah*. Since the Temple no longer stands and no sacrifices are served at our *seder* tables, the laws of ritual purity do not apply. Nevertheless, the symbolism associated with immersion into the *mikvah* is still potent and profitable for our learning.

Many sects of Judaism still practice immersion before festivals. For believers, Yeshua is the spiritual *mikvah* into which we are immersed. Therefore, it is appropriate to enter into a *mikvah* before God's Passover as a remembrance of the days of the Temple and as an acknowledgement of our cleansing in Yeshua.

This is all the more reason why the *mikvah* ritual is appropriate. Passover is a memorial or remembrance of what God has already done, yet we relive the experience year after year.

I encourage everyone to consider the following points in regard to participation in a ritual *mikvah* prior to conducting a Passover *seder*:

- ❧ The *mikvah* allows each of us to personally identify with the death, burial, and resurrection of the Messiah Yeshua.
- ❧ It allows each individual to physically connect with the renewed, sanctified life that we enter into during this time each year.
- ❧ It reminds us of the crossing of the Red Sea and the giving of the Torah at Sinai, when God told the people to wash in preparation for His presence at *Shavuot*.

The appropriate time to conduct the *mikvah* is before dusk on Nisan 14.

WASHING THE FEET

At His last *seder*, Yeshua gave us a powerful example of service, love, and humility by washing His disciples' feet. Yeshua Himself is our example. In John 13, He set a precedent on the night of His redemptive work:

> Then He poured water into the basin, and began to wash the disciples' feet and to wipe them with the towel with which He was girded. So He came to Simon Peter.
>
> He said to Him, "Lord, do You wash my feet?"
>
> Yeshua answered and said to him, "What I do you do not realize now, but you will understand hereafter."
>
> Peter said to Him, "Never shall You wash my feet!"
>
> Yeshua answered him, "If I do not wash you, you have no part with Me."

Simon Peter said to Him, "Lord, then wash not only my feet, but also my hands and my head."

Yeshua said to him, "He who has bathed needs only to wash his feet, but is completely clean; and you are clean, but not all of you." For He knew the one who was betraying Him; for this reason He said, "Not all of you are clean." So when He had washed their feet, and taken His garments and reclined at the table again, He said to them, "Do you know what I have done to you? You call Me Teacher and Lord; and you are right, for so I am. If I then, the Lord and the Teacher, washed your feet, you also ought to wash one another's feet. For I gave you an example that you also should do as I did to you. Truly, truly, I say to you, a slave is not greater than his master, nor is one who is sent greater than the one who sent him. If you know these things, you are blessed if you do them." (John 13:5–17)

The practice of washing feet arose from the need for traveling guests (wearing sandals) to clean their feet, upon entering the home, from the dirt that had gathered on their journey. Although times have changed and a physical cleaning is not necessary from a practical standpoint, the modeling of humility, service, and leadership that the Messiah offered through this demonstration is still applicable to our lives today. This act of service is a priceless tool that allows each of us to demonstrate the true heart of a servant. By washing one another's feet, we restore and build more intimate relationships.

Sabbath Issues

Equally important to honoring the appointed time of *Pesach* on its recognized day is honoring the *Shabbatot* and the mandates connected to them during the week of Unleavened Bread. We are not to keep Passover and then run off to work the next morning.

I believe that the *Shabbat* that follows Passover is specifically connected to Passover in order to allow extra time for the spiritual seed that was planted in us to germinate before we head back into our chaotic lives and lose sight of the work that God began in us the night before.

The command of *Shabbat* is to rest, to not go our own way, to cease. The *Shabbat* gives us time to reflect on our new spiritual reality. When preparing for Passover, it is imperative that we consider and prepare also for the Sabbaths that connect with it.

Even if Passover falls right after the weekly *Shabbat*—however difficult it may be—I believe that it is important that we do not violate the Sabbath in order to prepare for the *seder*. Instead, we should prepare a day ahead.

These occasions provide us with opportunities to be innovative and creative so that we are able to truly honor the commands of God's Torah. We can also find joy in reconciling the various challenges that need to be considered and, in the end, truly begin to understand what it means to enter God's rest.

Anything Else I Should Know?

The most important thing is that you set this time aside. You meet with your Maker. You relish the redemptive truths of this season and rejoice in the work of God in your life. These times are the seasons of our joy as the people of God.

Practically Employing this Haggadah

This *Haggadah* can be used in homes or in large-group settings. It works well on all levels. You will need to do some preparation work regardless of the venue. Here are some helpful suggestions.

- Advanced Household Preparation Ideas
    - Mark Passover on your calendar months in advance, and keep it in mind as you prepare for the *seder*. Remember not to plan business travel, special events, etc. just prior to the *seder*.
    - About six weeks ahead of time, start planning your *seder*. Make preparations for whom you will share the *seder* table with, where you will have your *seder*, and what time you will begin. Clearly communicate your intentions with everyone you

will be sharing Passover with, and make sure you are all on the same page about the special significance of the evening. Once you have agreed to the details, send out your invitations so that your guests can mark their calendars and be equally prepared.[37]

- About one month before Passover, start sorting and cleaning your home. I recommend one room at a time. My wife likes to spend several days on each room in order to do a complete and thorough job. You never can tell where those little bits of leaven crumbs will hide! You may want to take this time each year to move your furniture and perhaps even have the carpets cleaned.

- About two weeks prior to Passover, begin thinking about your menu. Consider what you will buy so you don't have to throw too much away just before Passover. Also, if you wish to dress up for the *seder*, begin looking for clothes now.

- The week before Passover should be a wrap-up week. During this time, you can begin preparing food, finish your cleaning, and completely rid your home of leaven.

- The night before: Take some time to seriously search your home for leaven (*Bedikat Chametz*) together as a family. This is a silent search and is intended to be carried out by the father of the home with full participation from all the children.

- Preparation for the *seder* service: The service is about an hour and a half long. Although it may be difficult, I suggest you do everything possible to ensure that people are able to participate without distractions in one complete setting. Preparation for this may include:

  - Telling children to be prepared to sit and participate in a lengthy service. You can provide crayons and coloring pages of the Exodus account if needed.

🙶 Having people eat a snack prior to coming, as the meal will be after the *seder* service.

🙶 Encouraging people to use the restroom prior to the *seder* service.

🙶 Having water provisions for people at the tables.

🙶 Have one individual serve as the host. This person will be the conductor of the service. This should be someone who reads clearly, loudly, and smoothly. He or she should also be well acquainted with the material, including the endnotes.

🙶 Depending on the size of the group, you will need to designate several "readers." These will be individuals who read at set times throughout the service. Again, it is suggested that you select people who can read clearly. I would advise that you highlight each reader's section in his or her personal *Haggadah* and write everyone's name by the particular section in the host's *Haggadah*. It is recommended that you give the readers their material in advance so they have time to familiarize themselves with their sections. I suggest you get as many people involved as readers as possible. It is important that everyone participates.

🙶 Hosts

🙶 Familiarize yourself with this material. Your comfort with it will come across to those who are participating and will enable them to more fully receive from your facilitation of this service.

🙶 The endnotes contain a wealth of information that will further enhance your knowledge of this material.

🙶 Try to create a contemplative environment during the consumption of the second cup. This time during the seder is meant to be a time of drawn out silence so that every member at your seder table has ample time to commune with Adonai regarding sin.

- All readers should be instructed to read:
  - Slowly
  - Deliberately
  - With emphasis
- Everyone should follow along in the *Haggadah* while others are reading.
- The table setting:
  - Simple is best. We use clear plastic cups with wine or grape juice. There are to be four per setting. The plate will have several spoonfuls of maror and several cracker-size sections of *matzah*. Everything should be set prior to the *seder* service. During the readings and the transitions to the partaking of the various elements and cups, you want to minimize distractions. Here is a sample of our *seder* plate.

- Eating the *Maror*
  - We have found it best to use grated horseradish root mixed with pre-pared horseradish sold in a jar. When the *maror* is eaten we recommend that it be eaten by itself.
- The accompanying audio CD contains:
  - Three Messianic-oriented songs written by Steve McConnell and performed by Ryan McCarthy. These songs work best for the thrust of this *Hag-*

gadah and are highly recommended. Please note that the playing time for the songs is roughly 24 minutes. We indicate where to insert these songs in the service if you choose to employ them.

- Three contemporary Christian-oriented songs. You may choose to use these songs as a substitute for the recommended Messianic songs if you are utilizing this *seder* to communicate the value and relevance of Passover to Christian friends and family who are unfamiliar or uncomfortable with Messianic terminology. We indicate where to insert these songs in the service if you choose to employ them.

- Carefully pronounced Hebrew prayers and traditional melodies for various parts of the service. These are meant to help the host learn the prayers, but they are not intended to be played during the *seder*. These are all indicated in the service.

- A dramatic retelling of the Exodus by D. Thomas Lancaster. This is primarily meant as a complement to the CD, to be played for young ones prior to the night of the *seder* in order to further familiarize them with the evening. It is not recommended that this retelling be used during the *seder* meal itself. Bumper music used with permission from Zemer Levav. Their Messianic music is highly recommended. Contact: *www.zemerlevav.org*

- Here are some suggestions for using the audio CDs:

  - Carefully select and prepare the songs you will utilize during the *seder*.

  - Have the CD in the CD player and queued, with volume levels adjusted. The host may select someone to be responsible for this function during the *seder*.

  - Plan smooth and effortless transitions between the songs and the reading of the *Haggadah*.

Songs

The following songs were carefully selected to integrate into this *Haggadah*, highlighting key principles and allowing for contemplative moments. Both Messianic and contemporary Christian songs are provided for individuals, congregations, and ministries to tailor the Passover Encounter service according to worship preference.

I would like to thank Ryan McCarthy for his responsive and professional work on all of these songs. Thank you for being part of the FFOZ team. I am so blessed to know that your talents are so vast. I am sure that the Father will use you in many ways to share the message of His Messiah and the Torah.

These songs are used with permission. The contemporary Christian songs were slightly altered to allow for usage of the name Yeshua. Both sets of songs provide opportunities for rich and heartfelt worship and contemplation.

- Messianic-Style Songs
    - Song #1 : The Pesach Song (We're Leaving)
    - Song #2 : The Lord Knows and Remembers
    - Song #3 : The Mikvah Song

- Contemporary Christian Songs
    - Song #4 : You Have Called Me
    - Song #5 : Redeemer, Savior, Friend
    - Song #6 : I Will Never Be the Same Again

The Pesach Song (We're Leaving)

Chorus:
We're leaving, leaving Mitzraim to worship our holy King.
We follow our Redeemer.
God leads us to the land He promised and we're leaving tonight.

Ten times the Pharaoh had his chance, and nine times he said no.
But now he's come to face the power of God—he begs for us to go.
Four hundred years in slavery to Pharaoh and his throne
Are coming to a halt tonight—our God is coming to take us home.
He requires of us a sacrifice, for only blood atones.
And on the doorposts of our dwelling place, it marks us as His own.
This lamb that we have slain tonight was offered in our place.
Staff in hand we stand prepared to leave—we must eat this meal in
haste. (chorus)

Now a three-day journey faces us from Ramses to Sukkot.
And from that moment God is with us, in clouds of fire and of smoke.
But Pharaoh's army seeks our life; Moses lifts his holy hands.
We have mikvah in the sea of reeds, leaving Egypt where they stand.
(chorus)

THE LORD KNOWS AND REMEMBERS

You've washed us clean, Holy Lamb.
You bore our shame, God of Abraham.
Your word is true and Your promise is sure,
And by Your grace we will live with You forever, oh Lord.

Oh Lord, I'm undone, I'm ashamed by all I've done.
And it hurts to think I'd grieve Your heart.
But You say, "Take My hand, little one—I understand."
And I as I hold Your hand I behold the scars
From the nails so undeserved
That gave me hope and Your assurance
That I am Yours indeed.

Now if You, oh Lord, kept a record of our sins,
Surely none of us could stand.
And You knew all along and so before the world was formed,
You Yourself would be salvation's plan.
In time, the spring of Living Water
Would go—like a lamb unto the slaughter—
To pay our debt in full.

Oh Lord, it's true, we should not sin,
For all who live in You are truly new creations.
But Lord, You say, if we should fall,
We need only see it as You do,
Running to, and not from You.
For the Lord knows how we're formed,
He remembers we are dust.

The Mikvah Song

What's in the past, what lies ahead,
Is hidden in this pool of our Father's tears.
And that's our hope, the old man is gone;
The new man is seated with Messiah in the heavenlies.
Lord, it breaks my heart to see the sin that lives in me.
But I know this memory is not real.
So when sin makes a plea for a small victory,
I know better now, I know the mystery!
So all praise to our God the Father of our Lord
By His mercy we are born again!
And our faith is alive—it's a gift that cannot die
Our names are found in His book of life!
By the Mikvah we've identified with the death and rising of Messiah.
Now we are sanctified.
We're set apart for good works and righteousness in Yeshua.
And every word He said is true,
So we are creatures who are born anew—in Him.
To walk by faith and not by sight
And know the law of God is our delight.
This is not a thing we've done on our own.
It's the work of God alone.

You Have Called Me

Eric Nuzum-Thomason

Chorus:
Lord, light a fire again, I feel new life begin,
I'll stand and testify; Lord, new strength abounds in me,
Yeshua* set me free, I am brand new.

You have called me to Your table,
You have called me by name;
You know the hunger within my heart,
I don't want to be the same.

Lord, let Your power grow
Inside my heart, I know,
I will be changed;
Lord, Your glory will be shown,
My life is not my own,
I give it to You.
I will seek You with all I am,
I will find You in that secret place;
Don't hide Your face from me,
When I seek You I will find You.

Lord, let Your power grow
Inside my heart, I know,
I will be changed;
Lord, Your glory will be shown,
My life is not my own,
I give it to You.

* The original version uses "revival"
in the chorus instead of "Yeshua."

REDEEMER, SAVIOR, FRIEND

Darrell Evans, Chris Springer
©1999 Integrity's Hosanna! Music/ASCAP & Integrity's Praise! Music/BMI
c/o Integrity Media, Inc., 1000 Cody Road, Mobile, AL 36695

I know You had me on Your mind
When You climbed up on that hill;
For You saw me with eternal eyes,
While I was yet in sin;
Redeemer, Savior, Friend.

Every stripe upon Your battered back,
Every thorn that pierced Your brow;
Every nail drove deep through guiltless hands,
Said that Your love knows no end;
Redeemer, Savior, Friend.

Redeemer, redeem my heart again;
Savior, come and shelter me from sin;
You're familiar with my weakness,
Devoted to the end;
Redeemer, Savior, Friend.

So the grace You pour upon my life,
Will return to You in praise;
And I'll gladly lay down all my crowns,
For the name by which I'm saved;
Redeemer, Savior, Friend.

I Will Never Be the Same Again

Geoffrey Bullock

I will never be the same again;
I can never return, I've closed the door;
I'll walk the path, I'll run the race,
And I will never be the same again.
(Repeat)

Fall like fire, soak like rain,
Flow like mighty waters again and again;
Sweep away the darkness, burn away the chaff,
And let the flame burn to glorify Your name.

There are higher heights, there are deeper seas;
Whatever you need to do, Lord, do it in me;
The glory of God fills my life,
And I will never be the same again.

Glossary of Terms

Adonai
    God's name, the Lord

Bedikat Chametz
    The traditional custom of searching for leaven

Chag ha'aviv
    Another name for Passover; literally, "holiday" (*chag*) of "the spring" (*ha aviv*)

Chag HaMatzot
    Another name for the Feast of Unleavened Bread; literally, "holiday" (*chag*) of "the unleavened bread" (*ha matzah*)

Chametz
    Leaven, which is symbolic for sin

Dayeinu
    "It would have been enough!" This is a refrain from a popular *seder* song.

Haggadah
    Passover instructional booklet; literally, "the telling"

Hagadot
    Plural of *Haggadah*

Leaven
    Substance used in cooking to make bread rise (Exodus 12:15); symbol for sin (1 Corinthians 5:7)

Maror
    Bitter herbs (Exodus 12:8)

Matzah
    Bread made without leaven (Exodus 12:8)

Matzot
    Plural of *matzah*

Mikvah
 Ritual immersion used for purification; symbolic of baptism

Mitzrayim
 Egypt; symbolic of Satan

Mitzvot
 Good deeds; literally, "commandments"

Moadim
 The feasts of the Lord outlined in Leviticus 23; plural of *moed*

Moed
 Appointed time

Omer
 Literally, a measure of barely; used in conjunction with "counting the omer" (the 49 days between Passover and Pentecost)

Pesach
 Passover, the feast that commemorates the Exodus from Egypt (Exodus 12)

Seder
 Traditional meal and liturgy in the home that celebrates Passover; literally, "order"

Shabbat
 Sabbath

Shavuot
 Pentecost, the biblical feast that comes seven weeks after Passover and that coincides with the events of Acts 2

Sukkah
 A booth, tent, or tabernacle

Sukkot
 Feast of Tabernacles or Booths; the final, seven-day, joy-filled festival that foreshadows Messiah dwelling on earth; plural of *sukkah*

Torah
 The five books of Moses; literally, "instruction," sometimes translated "law"

Yeshua
 Jesus; literally, "salvation"

Yom Kippur
 Day of Atonement

Endnotes

1. Leviticus 23 outlines the *moadim* (appointed times) of God for His people. They are the seventh-day Sabbath (*Shabbat)*, Passover (*Pesach)*, Unleavened Bread *(Chag HaMatzot)*, The Counting (*Omer*), Pentecost *(Shavuot)*, Feast of Trumpets (*Yom Teruah*), Day of Atonement *(Yom Kippur),* and the Feast of Tabernacles *(Sukkot).* There is also a reference to *Purim* as a time of remembrance in the book of Esther and allusions to the acknowledgment and monthly sighting of the New Moon *(Rosh Chodesh)* as an appointment.

2. "Therefore no one is to act as your judge in regard to food or drink or in respect to a festival or a new moon or a Sabbath day—things which are a [*mere*] shadow of what is to come; but the substance belongs to Messiah." (Colossians 2:16–17) Note: the word 'mere' is an insertion of the translators. It is neither found nor implied in the original Greek text.

3. "So then, brethren, we are under obligation, not to the flesh, to live according to the flesh—for if you are living according to the flesh, you must die; but if by the Spirit you are putting to death the deeds of the body, you will live." (Romans 8:12–13)

4. "…in humility receive the word implanted, which is able to save your souls." (James 1:21)

5. This is a teaching in and of itself—far too vast for this short note. However, to understand my point, please read the revival under Nehemiah (Nehemiah 8:1–12) as well as the revival connected to the festival of *Shavuot* in the book of Acts. Walter C. Kaiser Jr. has a fascinating book titled *Quest for Renewal*, in which he outlines multiple revivals in the Tanach (Old Testament). In this work he connects revivals in the history of Israel directly to the rededication and repentance to the commandments of the Torah.

6. *Mitzrayim* = Egypt. Egypt is often equated to our old nature, our flesh.

7. *At Our Rebbes' Table*, Rabbi Eli Touger, Sichos in English (Brooklyn, NY, 1995).

8. One example of many is found in the simple greeting "*Shabbat Shalom,*" spoken by the clerk at the bank on Tuesday morning, knowing that he will not see you again until next Tuesday after the weekly *Shabbat* that is still four days away.

9. Please contact FFOZ for a unique circular calendar that enables one to clearly anticipate God's *moadim* at a glance. It is an invaluable resource for families, communities, and individuals who desire to live out their faith and keep the Father's appointed times.

[10] This is a reference to Colossians 2:16–17. This is a powerful verse that is usually used by opponents of the honoring of God's biblical calendar. They often use the term *shadow* as a negative. However, I believe that shadows represent the presence of something real—in this analogy, the Messiah. Shadows also represent the shape of something real—although dimly, when we honor the appointed times we are forming the "shadow" of the presence of the Master, as they all point to and speak of Him.

[11] "I am the LORD your God, who brought you out of Egypt, out of the land of slavery …Remember the Sabbath day to keep it holy." (Exodus 20:2, 8) The whole covenant is predicated on the fact that the Lord brought His people out of captivity.

[12] *Pesach: Birth and Rebirth,* (Orthodox) Rabbi Pinchas Stolper (New York: Orthodox Union, May 6, 1997), www.ou.org.

[13] I would like to quote briefly from an excellent article written by my wife titled "A Feather Story," as it links the removal of leaven from the home to the cleansing of one's heart. "I wish that I could take away the *chametz* of our lives as easily as I can that of the home. As *Abba,* I am responsible to see to it that leaven does not build up in the lives of our family from year to year. My heart is saddened at this time every year because I wish I wouldn't find any leaven at all in the house. Come, let's take the leaven to the fire and cast it away from our lives. Let us look to the Creator, the Holy One, blessed be He, for cleansing and utter consumption of our sin." *messiah magazine*, issue #85, Vayikra 5765, pp. 18–19.

[14] The timing of the giving of the covenant on *Shavuot* at Mt. Sinai is more a matter of tradition than fact. However, in my opinion, the timing of the giving of the commandments was relatively close to the time of Shavu'ot. Exodus 19:1 states, "In the third month after the sons of Israel had gone out of the land of Egypt, on that very day they came into the wilderness of Sinai." The Exodus occurred in the first month. The covenant of Torah was given in or around the third month.

[15] I derive much of my thinking on this process from Psalm 51. For emphasis on the intrinsic nature of the spring feast in the processes of redemption, cleansing, maturity, and equipping, I have inserted titles of the biblical feasts into this short section of Psalm 51. I think this passage captures the heart of the cycle of sanctification. It states, "O God, according to Your lovingkindness; according to the greatness of Your compassion blot out my transgressions [Passover]. Wash me thoroughly from my iniquity and cleanse me from my sin [Unleavened Bread]. For I know my transgressions, and my sin is ever before me. Against You, You only, I have sinned and done what is evil in Your sight, so that You are justified when You speak and blameless when You judge. Behold, I was brought forth in iniquity, and in sin my mother conceived me. Behold, You desire truth in the innermost being, and in the hidden part You will make me know wisdom [Omer]. Purify me with hyssop, and I shall be clean; wash me, and I shall be whiter than snow [Passover]. Make me to hear joy and gladness, let the bones which You have broken rejoice. Hide Your face from my sins and blot out all my iniquities [Passover].Create in me a clean heart [Unleavened

Bread], O God, and renew a steadfast spirit within me. Do not cast me away from Your presence and do not take Your Holy Spirit from me. Restore to me the joy of Your salvation and sustain me with a willing spirit [Omer]. Then I will teach transgressors Your ways, and sinners will be converted to You [Shavuot]. (Psalm 51:1–13)

[16] See Revelation 20:12–15.

[17] Essentially this *Haggadah* has a specific purpose and I felt that certain extrabiblical traditions either slowed the service down or missed the purpose of this particular telling. I do recognize that the picking and choosing of various extrabiblical traditions can be confusing to those of us who are well acquainted with all the various traditions, but many will not realize their absence. To be sure, my selection process was not done to speak against those other traditions; rather, it was to enable this *Haggadah* to highlight the issues of sanctification, redemption, deliverance, and hope. It is my contention that there are hundreds of *Haggadot* that highlight those important traditions in a far more meaningful and significant way than what I would be able to do, and the redundancy is unnecessary.

[18] "Now this day will be a memorial to you," says Exodus 12:14. We are instructed to keep the Passover and Unleavened Bread as a "memorial" of the Exodus from Egypt.

[19] From a perspective of history, this instructional booklet (*Haggadah*) would be considered very traditional; however, when looking at it in comparison with most traditional *Haggadot*, this one is anything but traditional, primarily because of its focus on the Messiah and His historical and eternal work in our lives.

[20] For additional teaching see Hegg, "I am Adonai and I Will…" Issue 68, *Bikurei Tziyon*, First Fruits of Zion. Note: *Bikurei Tziyon* is now *messiah magazine*. The four cups are clearly a rabbinic invention. "The obligation to drink four cups of wine was another rabbinic provision which was introduced, most likely, within several decades after the destruction of the temple. Some modern scholars assume that this is a custom that had already been practiced in the temple era. There seems to be no evidence to support such an assumption. The Talmud states that the custom is of rabbinic origin." (*Pesachim* 109b) *The Biblical and Historical Background of the Jewish Holy Days*, Abraham P. Bloch

[21] In some believing circles, when a *moed* is observed, it is typically for outreach, cultural expression, or teaching purposes rather than exploring the natural, continuous discipleship and growth potential unique to each of God's appointed times. Remember, God's *moadim* are not simply footnotes in the lifestyle of the redeemed or additions to the believer's life; rather, they are the very height of our intimacy with and worship of the Messiah. Each appointment is specifically designed and used by the Master to bring us into a greater knowledge of Him.

[22] The traditional liturgy for starting the weekly Shabbat.

[23] The traditional liturgy for ending Shabbat.

²⁴ This is technical but important. The timing of the *Pesach* is specific. The Scriptures refer to this time as "twilight." It is that moment when the sun goes down, yet there still is a haze of light. It is a short window of time—a time of transition. (See Exodus 12:6, 18; Leviticus 23:5; Numbers 9:3, 5; 28:16; Joshua 5:10; Ezekiel 45:21; Ezra 6:19; 2 Chronicles 35:1.)

²⁵ The phrase "Let My people go, that they may serve Me" is repeated over and over throughout the Exodus account. "And afterward Moses and Aaron came and said to Pharaoh, 'Thus says the LORD, the God of Israel, 'Let My people go that they may celebrate a feast to Me in the wilderness.' ' " (Exodus 5:1) The additional references in Exodus 7:16, 8:1, 8:20, 9:1, 9:13, and 10:3 all contain the phrase "Let My people go," which is an appeal for intimacy and relationship. This phrase is carried over to each of us as redeemed individuals because God desires to bring us into a place of wholeness so that we may worship Him unhindered. He has called us out from darkness to light.

²⁶ Did Yeshua violate the Torah by asking His disciples to drink blood? In FFOZ's commentary in Torah Club Volume 4 on John 6:60–66, D. Thomas Lancaster states, "In Yeshua's day, the annual Passover imagery of eating the Passover lamb and drinking the four cups of the 'blood of grapes' at the Passover *seder* provided a matrix of imagery for Him to draw from. For us, without temple and without sacrifice, such metaphoric language is by necessity confined to the context of sacrament, communion and the Lord's Supper. Without the broader imagery of Passover to provide context, the line between figurative and literal is quickly blurred. But is it possible that the Jewish congregation in the synagogue at Capernaum actually took Yeshua literally and understood Him to be suggesting cannibalism? On the contrary, all indications from Jewish literature point to a literate society, deftly handling and manipulating metaphor, sorting and reassigning symbolism much more capably than we. Immersed since childhood in the poetry of the Hebrew Scriptures, it is hardly a wonder that the Jews of the Capernaum synagogue were far more literate than we and far better equipped to think abstractly than the average modern reader. We have typically assumed that they were offended because of the cannibalistic imagery. After all, the Torah forbids the consumption of blood. But in Hebrew literature, the blood of grapes is idiomatic for wine. ("Blood of grapes" is a virtually universal metaphor for wine.) That being said, how is it that so many of His disciples were offended at the Bread of Life discourse? Obviously it was not the eating and drinking of His body that offended them, for that much was obviously supposed to be taken figuratively. After the question in verse 52, Yeshua answered them by moving the flesh-eating/blood-drinking metaphor to the spiritual plane of bread descending from heaven. It was His claim of descent from heaven that troubled them. As in verse 42, they knew better. They knew He did not descend from heaven. His claim to have been with God and to have come to earth left them frustrated and uncertain. They were frustrated that He kept talking like this and were uncertain about His sanity. On hearing that Yeshua regarded Himself as descended from heaven, many of His disciples said, "This is a hard teaching. Who can accept it?" (John 5:60). Yeshua understood that they were having difficulty with the notion that He had descended from heaven. After all, there were some there

who had known Him since He was a child. But they had known only His "flesh"; that is, His body. They had not perceived His true spiritual essence. He corrected them, saying, "The flesh profits nothing" (v. 63) and *What then if you see the Son of Man ascending to where He was before?*" (v. 62) All this spiritual mumbo-jumbo was too much for the pragmatic Galileans. John sadly said, "As a result of this many of His disciples withdrew and were not walking with Him anymore." (v. 66) It is not the later theological error of transubstantiation that gave them pause; it was the mystery of the incarnation that turned them away."

[27] I would like to refer the reader to FFOZ's works on the issue of identity and participation in and as Israel. *The Mystery of the Gospel* by D. Thomas Lancaster and *FellowHeirs* by Tim Hegg are comprehensive works in the area of inclusion in Israel through adoption and by the eternal work of the Messiah. See *www.ffoz.org* for more information.

[28] "You shall remember that you were a slave in the land of Egypt, and the LORD your God brought you out of there by a mighty hand and by an outstretched arm; therefore the LORD your God commanded you to observe the Sabbath day." (Deuteronomy 5:15)

The teachers of Israel considered this command to mean that every Israelite should consider himself to be personally freed from Egypt by God. The salvation of Israel was so intrinsic to the covenant that even converts were to regard themselves as having been freed from Egypt along with all Israel. The same is true for believers. Once we are in Messiah, we are children of Abraham according to the promise. We are brought near to God and to the covenants and promises of Israel through Christ's work. Paul repeatedly taught that there was one family of God, not two, and that the Gentiles coming to faith had joined the "commonwealth of Israel," having been "brought near" (Ephesians 2:11–13) by faith in Yeshua. He reveled in the joy of Gentiles being "fellow heirs," "fellow citizens," "fellow members of the household of God," and "fellow partakers of the promise" (Ephesians 2:19; 3:6).

We are adopted into the commonwealth of Israel. As such we too can remember that we were in bondage to the Pharaoh of this world, and with a mighty hand and outstretched arm God freed us from the slavery of sin and set us free to live a life of righteousness. The celebration of Passover is a means by which we are to remember our salvation. It gives us a picture of our salvation.

[29] "As obedient children, do not be conformed to the former lusts *which were yours* in your ignorance, but like the Holy One who called you, be holy yourselves also in all *your* behavior; because it is written, "YOU SHALL BE HOLY, FOR I AM HOLY." (1 Peter 1:14–16)

[30] All of the technical aspects required in order to fulfill the specifications of Passover are impossible today because there is no longer a temple in Jerusalem at which one can offer a sacrificial lamb (actually called "the *pesach*" in the Hebrew Scriptures). However, the *seder* service provides a means for individual families to observe the mandate first to tell the redemption story and then to eat the *maror* and unleavened bread as commanded.

[31] "They shall eat the flesh that *same* night, roasted with fire, and they shall eat it with unleavened bread and bitter herbs [*maror*]." (Exodus 12:8)

[32] Exodus 13:8

[33] Deuteronomy 6:23

[34] Exodus 14:13

[35] Exodus 15:1–21

[36] *Dayeinu* means "It would have been enough." To demonstrate all the positive consequences of choosing God, *Haggadot* lists all the good that God has done for His people through history. *Dayeinu* has fifteen stanzas, fifteen aspects, fifteen gifts. The first five involve leaving the lowliness of enslavement to our bodies. The second five describe miracles—i.e., how God changes nature. The last five show closeness to God. (Derived from commentary on *www.aish.com*.)

[37] First Fruits of Zion has created invitations that match the theme of "Passover Encounter" and are available for purchase. Quantities and prices vary. Call 800–775–4807 for more information or to order.

[38] On a practical level, the prohibition on an uncircumcised person eating the Passover (*pesach*) does not apply because there is no Passover sacrifice made today. There is absolutely no prohibition on an uncircumcised person partaking of the *matzah*, the bitter herbs, or the *seder* cups. Therefore, everyone should feel welcome at the table. Even though the prohibition is not relevant in today's world, it does teach us some deeper lessons.

Additional Resources

Bible Study Programs, Books and Teachings

Do you want to understand God's Word in its historical, cultural and linguistic context? First Fruits of Zion resources will help you better understand the Bible.

ᴥ Restorahtion

A new book by D. Thomas Lancaster. This easy-to-read introduction to the Jewish roots of Christianity picks up where *Holy Cow!* leaves off. It provides a fresh look at the Torah while challenging centuries of misinterpretation and neglect.

ᴥ Messiah magazine

Published five times a year, each full-color issue provides fresh articles and perspectives about our Torah-observant Messiah, the grace we have in Him, and the truth He taught. For more information or to subscribe, visit *www.messiahmagazine.org.*

ᴥ The Letter Writer

Paul's Background and Torah Perspective. This book by Tim Hegg challenges traditional Christian viewpoints of Paul, his message, and the foundation of his theological approach. Through this book, Hegg re-establishes a biblical, historical and cultural understanding of Paul—the Torah observant Apostle.

◣ Fellowheirs

Jews & Gentiles Together in the Family of God. This book by Tim Hegg seeks the biblical perspective on identity within the family of God. Is the Torah for all of God's children, or is it only for Jews? Who are the people the Torah refers to as "strangers"? Do Gentile believers have a legitimate place in Messianic Communities? FellowHeirs answers these questions and more.

◣ The Mystery of the Gospel

Jew and Gentile and the Eternal Purpose of God. This book by D. Thomas Lancaster, addresses the question of Jewish/Gentile relationships within the body of Messiah. In this friendly, easy to read, narrative style, the author works through the Apostle Paul's rabbinic scholarship to piece together the deep mystery of the Messiah. Ultimately, that mystery is about the identity of Gentile believers and their relationship to Israel through the Messiah.

◣ Holy Cow!

Does God Care about What We Eat? Join *messiah magazine* editor and best-selling author Hope Egan on her personal journey through what the Bible says about eating meat. The author helps you see how science and Scripture brilliantly intertwine. Promoting neither legalism nor vegetarianism, Holy Cow! gently challenges you to take a fresh look at how you live out your faith!

PLUS : **Man Alive! There's More!** Written by D. Thomas Lancaster, Man Alive! delves further into some of the most challenging Scripture passages mentioned in the main part of this book. Fasten your seatbelts and get out your Bibles; this may be the richest Scripture study you have ever experienced.

❧ HaYesod

This 14-week video Bible study delves into the Hebraic roots of Christianity and is ideal for group teaching or personal study. For more information visit *www.hayesod.org* or call 800–775–4807 and request a HaYesod info pack.

❧ Torah Club

Study the Torah, the Gospels and Acts passage-by-passage from within the context of Torah and classical Judaism. It is FFOZ's most comprehensive resource for providing biblical context. Visit *www.torahclub.org* or call toll free 800–775–4807 to request a brochure.

WWW.FFOZ.ORG

For more information about these and other FFOZ books, magazines and multi-media products, or to download free samples, please visit *www.ffoz.org* or call toll free 800–775–4807.

❧ FREE Weekly Teaching

FFOZ provides subscribers a free weekly e-mail teaching that focuses on Messiah and Torah. To see a sample edition or to sign up, go to *www.ffoz.org/edrash*.

PASSOVER ENCOUNTER

The following items, designed to be used with this book, can be purchased from First Fruits of Zion.

- ❧ Passover Encounter CD (includes Songs, Hebrew helps, and a dramatic telling of the Exodus)
- ❧ Seder Invitation and Event Cards

If you desire to host a Passover Encounter seder for a large group, FFOZ can assist you with advertising and promotion.